D1319766

Our Town

The Skin of Our Teeth

"Amid the encircling gloom of the depression and preparations for war, a quiet man with an enormous fund of knowledge spoke some inspired words about the human race. He was Thornton Wilder." So Brooks Atkinson described Wilder, and defined the context in which Wilder's two Pulitzer Prize-winning plays were written.

When *Our Town* was first produced in 1938, Wilder was forty-one years old, an accomplished and popular novelist. As a playwright, he wondered why the contemporary theatre had failed to tap the universal themes so well understood by the classical Greeks, and he was determined, as he said of *Our Town*, "to find a value above all price for the smallest events of our daily life."

Born in Madison, Wisconsin, in 1897, the son of a clergyman, Wilder accompanied his father to China when the latter was sent by President Theodore Roosevelt as consul general to Shanghai and Hong Kong. Upon his return to the United States, young Wilder attended school in California, and in due course received his B.A. degree from Yale in 1920.

His career as a writer dates, in part, from the experiences he had as a postgraduate student at the American Academy in Rome. *The Cabala*, Wilder's first novel, was published in 1926 and was moderately well received by both the critics and the public. The next year, *The Bridge of San Luis Rey* catapulted Wilder to a position of international fame, selling more than 100,000 copies its first year in print, and requiring thirteen printings to satisfy public demand in England. In 1928 *The Bridge of San Luis Rey* received the Pulitzer Prize for Fiction.

In 1930, while teaching English at the University of Chicago, Wilder published his third novel, *The Woman of Andros*, and in 1931 he finished his second collection of one-act plays, *The Long Christmas Dinner*.

Wilder's success as a novelist did not interfere with his desire to write plays. For some years before the first production of *Our Town,* he had been working in the theatre, and was becoming more and more convinced that contemporary theatre was failing to reach beneath the surface of life. It lacked the power of myth, he thought, "the recollection within us," as he put it. A good play should do more than stimulate passing emotions; it should touch the truth.

Even as Hitler prepared to annex Czechoslovakia, Wilder held fast to his belief that individuals, families, and communities had within them the power to resist the devastating forces that were at large in the world. *Our Town* opened in New York on February 4, 1938, at the Henry Miller Theatre, to mixed reviews. But after the audiences became adjusted to Wilder's nearly empty stage and had overcome the surprise occasioned by the playwright's simple language, the play ran for 336 performances and became a classic.

By November 1942, the month Fredric March and Tallulah Bankhead opened in *The Skin of Our Teeth*, the war had gone from bad to worse, and the mood on Broadway, as elsewhere, was grim. In 1942 General MacArthur retreated from the Philippines, and the tiny island of Guadalcanal became a household word across America. But here was Thornton Wilder, speaking through his character Mrs. Antrobus: "I could live for seventy years in a cellar and make soup of grass and bark, without ever doubting that this world has a work to do and will do it."

Thornton Wilder's plays have become, as Brooks Atkinson has said, "a permanent part of the American mythology," and this has happened because Wilder was able to show us more than we thought we had. He led us—wisely and well—to "the recollection within us."

The Editors

Books by Thornton Wilder

PLAYS

The Trumpet Shall Sound
The Angel That Troubled the Waters and Other Plays
The Long Christmas Dinner and Other Plays
Our Town
The Merchant of Yonkers *(revised as* The Matchmaker*)*
The Skin of Our Teeth
The Alcestiad
Plays for Bleecker Street

NOVELS

The Cabala
The Bridge of San Luis Rey
The Woman of Andros
Heaven's My Destination
The Ides of March
The Eighth Day
Theophilus North

NONFICTION

American Characteristics and Other Essays

The Pulitzer Prize for Drama 1938

Our Town

The Pulitzer Prize for Drama 1943

The Skin of Our Teeth

Illustrated by
Alan E. Cober

THE FRANKLIN LIBRARY
Franklin Center, Pennsylvania

Professionals and amateurs are hereby warned that OUR TOWN and THE SKIN OF OUR TEETH, being fully protected under the Copyright Laws of the United States of America and all other countries of the Berne and Universal Copyright Conventions, are subject to royalty. All rights, including but not limited to, professional, amateur, recording, motion picture, recitation, lecturing, public reading, radio and television broadcasting, and the rights of translation into foreign languages are strictly reserved, and permission for them must be secured in writing from the Author's agent. All inquiries should be addressed to Harold Freedman, Brandt & Brandt Dramatic Department, Inc., 1501 Broadway, New York, N.Y. 10036.

OUR TOWN: Copyright © 1938, 1957 by Thornton Wilder. THE SKIN OF OUR TEETH: Copyright 1942 by Thornton Wilder. Published by arrangement with Harper & Row, Publishers, Inc. Special contents copyright © 1983 The Franklin Library. Printed in the United States of America.

✧ ✧ ✧ ✧ ✧ ✧ ✧ ✧ ✧ ✧

Contents

Our Town

A Play in Three Acts

To Alexander Woollcott
of Castleton Township, Rutland County, Vermont

The first performance of this play took place at the McCarter Theatre, Princeton, New Jersey, on January 22, 1938. The first New York performance was at the Henry Miller Theatre, February 4, 1938. It was produced and directed by Jed Harris. The technical director was Raymond Sovey; the costumes were designed by Madame Hélène Pons. The role of the Stage Manager was played by Frank Craven. The Gibbs family were played by Jay Fassett, Evelyn Varden, John Craven, and Marilyn Erskine; the Webb family by Thomas Ross, Helen Carew, Martha Scott (as Emily), and Charles Wiley, Jr. Mrs. Soames was played by Doro Merande; Simon Stimson by Philip Coolidge.

Characters

In the order of their appearance

STAGE MANAGER
DR. GIBBS
MRS. GIBBS
MRS. WEBB
JOE CROWELL, JR.
HOWIE NEWSOME
GEORGE GIBBS
REBECCA GIBBS
WALLY WEBB
EMILY WEBB
PROFESSOR WILLARD
MR. WEBB
WOMAN IN THE BALCONY
MAN IN THE AUDITORIUM
LADY IN A BOX
SIMON STIMSON
MRS. SOAMES
CONSTABLE WARREN
SI CROWELL
THREE BASEBALL PLAYERS
JOE STODDARD
SAM CRAIG
THE DEAD

The entire play takes place in
Grover's Corners, New Hampshire.

AEC

Act One

No curtain.
No scenery.
The audience, arriving, sees an empty stage in half-light.
Presently the STAGE MANAGER, *hat on and pipe in mouth, enters and begins placing a table and three chairs downstage left, and a table and three chairs downstage right. He also places a low bench at the corner of what will be the Webb house, left.*
"Left" and "right" are from the point of view of the actor facing the audience. "Up" is toward the back wall.
As the houselights go down he has finished setting the stage and, leaning against the right proscenium pillar, watches the late arrivals in the audience.

When the auditorium is in complete darkness he speaks.

STAGE MANAGER:

This play is called "Our Town." It was written by Thornton Wilder; produced and directed by A. . . . (or: produced by A. . . .; directed by B. . . .). In it you will see Miss C. . . .; Miss D. . . .; Miss E. . . .; and Mr. F. . . .; Mr. G. . . .; Mr. H. . . .; and many others. The name of the town is Grover's Corners, New Hampshire—just across the Massachusetts line: latitude 42 degrees 40 minutes; longitude 70 degrees 37 minutes. The First Act shows a day in our town. The day is May 7, 1901. The time is just before dawn.

A rooster crows.

The sky is beginning to show some streaks of light over in the east there, behind our mount'in.

The morning star always gets wonderful bright the minute before it has to go, —doesn't it?

He stares at it for a moment, then goes upstage.

Well, I'd better show you how our town lies. Up here—

That is: parallel with the back wall.

is Main Street. Way back there is the railway station; tracks go that way. Polish Town's across the tracks, and some Canuck families.

Toward the left.

Over there is the Congregational Church; across the street's the Presbyterian.

Methodist and Unitarian are over there.

Baptist is down in the holla' by the river.

Catholic Church is over beyond the tracks.

Here's the Town Hall and Post Office combined; jail's in the basement.

Bryan once made a speech from these very steps here.

Along here's a row of stores. Hitching posts and horse blocks in front of them. First automobile's going to come along in about five years—belonged to Banker Cartwright, our richest citizen . . . lives in the big white house up on the hill.

Here's the grocery store and here's Mr. Morgan's drugstore. Most everybody in town manages to look into those two stores once a day.

Public School's over yonder. High School's still farther over. Quarter of nine mornings, noontimes, and three o'clock afternoons, the hull town can hear the yelling and screaming from those school yards.

He approaches the table and chairs downstage right.

This is our doctor's house, —Doc Gibbs'. This is the back door.

Two arched trellises, covered with vines and flowers, are pushed out, one by each proscenium pillar.

There's some scenery for those who think they have to have scenery.

This is Mrs. Gibbs' garden. Corn . . . peas . . . beans . . . hollyhocks . . . heliotrope . . . and a lot of burdock.

Crosses the stage.

In those days our newspaper come out twice a week—the Grover's Corners *Sentinel*—and this is Editor Webb's house.

And this is Mrs. Webb's garden.

Just like Mrs. Gibbs', only it's got a lot of sunflowers, too.

He looks upward, center stage.

Right here . . . 's a big butternut tree.

He returns to his place by the right proscenium pillar and looks at the audience for a minute.

Nice town, y'know what I mean?

Nobody very remarkable ever come out of it, s'far as we know.

The earliest tombstones in the cemetery up there on the mountain say 1670–1680—they're Grovers and Cartwrights and Gibbses and Herseys—same names as are around here now.

Well, as I said: it's about dawn.

The only lights on in town are in a cottage over by the

tracks where a Polish mother's just had twins. And in the Joe Crowell house, where Joe Junior's getting up so as to deliver the paper. And in the depot, where Shorty Hawkins is gettin' ready to flag the 5:45 for Boston.

A train whistle is heard. The STAGE MANAGER *takes out his watch and nods.*

Naturally, out in the country—all around—there've been lights on for some time, what with milkin's and so on. But town people sleep late.

So—another day's begun.

There's Doc Gibbs comin' down Main Street now, comin' back from that baby case. And here's his wife comin' downstairs to get breakfast.

MRS. GIBBS, *a plump, pleasant woman in the middle thirties, comes "downstairs" right. She pulls up an—imaginary—window shade in her kitchen and starts to make a fire in her stove.*

Doc Gibbs died in 1930. The new hospital's named after him.

Mrs. Gibbs died first—long time ago, in fact. She went out to visit her daughter, Rebecca, who married an insurance man in Canton, Ohio, and died there—pneumonia—but her body was brought back here. She's up in the cemetery there now—in with a whole mess of Gibbses and Herseys— She was Julia Hersey 'fore she married Doc Gibbs in the Congregational Church over there.

In our town we like to know the facts about everybody.

There's Mrs. Webb, coming downstairs to get her breakfast, too.

MRS. WEBB, *a thin, serious, crisp woman, has entered her kitchen, left, tying on an apron. She goes through the motions of putting wood into a stove, lighting it, and preparing breakfast.*

DR. GIBBS *has been coming along Main Street from the left. At the point where he would turn to approach his house, he stops, sets down his imaginary black bag, takes off his hat, and rubs his face with fatigue, using an enormous handkerchief.*

—That's Doc Gibbs. Got that call at half past one this morning.
And there comes Joe Crowell, Jr., delivering Mr. Webb's *Sentinel*.

Suddenly, JOE CROWELL, JR., *eleven, starts down Main Street from the right, hurling imaginary newspapers into doorways.*

JOE CROWELL, JR.:

Morning, Doc Gibbs.

DR. GIBBS:

Morning, Joe.

JOE CROWELL, JR.:

Somebody been sick, Doc?

DR. GIBBS:

No. Just some twins born over in Polish Town.

JOE CROWELL, JR.:

Do you want your paper now?

DR. GIBBS:

Yes, I'll take it. —Anything serious goin' on in the world since Wednesday?

JOE CROWELL, JR.:

Yessir. My schoolteacher, Miss Foster, 's getting married to a fella over in Concord.

DR. GIBBS:

I declare. —How do you boys feel about that?

JOE CROWELL, JR.:

Well, of course, it's none of my business—but I think if a person starts out to be a teacher, she ought to stay one.

DR. GIBBS:

How's your knee, Joe?

JOE CROWELL, JR.:

Fine, Doc, I never think about it at all. Only like you said, it always tells me when it's going to rain.

DR. GIBBS:

What's it telling you today? Goin' to rain?

JOE CROWELL, JR.:

No, sir.

DR. GIBBS:

Sure?

JOE CROWELL, JR.:

Yessir.

DR. GIBBS:

Knee ever make a mistake?

JOE CROWELL, JR.:

No, sir.

JOE *goes off.* DR. GIBBS *stands reading his paper.*

STAGE MANAGER:

Want to tell you something about that boy Joe Crowell there. Joe was awful bright—graduated from high school here, head of his class. So he got a scholarship to Massachusetts Tech. Graduated head of his class there, too. It was all wrote up in the Boston paper at the time. Goin' to be a great engineer, Joe was. But the war broke out and he died in France. —All that education for nothing.

HOWIE NEWSOME:

Off left.

Giddap, Bessie! What's the matter with you today?

STAGE MANAGER:

Here comes Howie Newsome, deliverin' the milk.

HOWIE NEWSOME, *about thirty, in overalls, comes along Main Street from the left, walking beside an invisible horse and wagon and carrying an imaginary rack with milk bottles. The sound of clinking milk bottles is heard. He leaves some bottles at Mrs. Webb's trellis, then, crossing the stage to Mrs. Gibbs', he stops center to talk to* DR. GIBBS.

HOWIE NEWSOME:

Morning, Doc.

DR. GIBBS:

Morning, Howie.

HOWIE NEWSOME:

Somebody sick?

DR. GIBBS:

Pair of twins over to Mrs. Goruslawski's.

HOWIE NEWSOME:

Twins, eh? This town's gettin' bigger every year.

DR. GIBBS:

Goin' to rain, Howie?

HOWIE NEWSOME:

No, no. Fine day—that'll burn through. Come on, Bessie.

DR. GIBBS:

Hello, Bessie.
He strokes the horse, which has remained up center.
How old is she, Howie?

HOWIE NEWSOME:

Going on seventeen. Bessie's all mixed up about the route ever since the Lockharts stopped takin' their quart of milk every day. She wants to leave 'em a quart just the same—keeps scolding me the hull trip.
He reaches Mrs. Gibbs' back door. She is waiting for him.

MRS. GIBBS:

Good morning, Howie.

HOWIE NEWSOME:

Morning, Mrs. Gibbs. Doc's just comin' down the street.

MRS. GIBBS:

Is he? Seems like you're late today.

HOWIE NEWSOME:

Yes. Somep'n went wrong with the separator. Don't know what 'twas.

He passes DR. GIBBS *up center.*

Doc!

DR. GIBBS:

Howie!

MRS. GIBBS:

Calling upstairs.

Children! Children! Time to get up.

HOWIE NEWSOME:

Come on, Bessie!

He goes off right.

MRS. GIBBS:

George! Rebecca!

DR. GIBBS *arrives at his back door and passes through the trellis into his house.*

Everything all right, Frank?

DR. GIBBS:

Yes. I declare—easy as kittens.

MRS. GIBBS:

Bacon'll be ready in a minute. Set down and drink your coffee.

You can catch a couple hours' sleep this morning, can't you?

DR. GIBBS:

Hm! . . . Mrs. Wentworth's coming at eleven. Guess I know what it's about, too. Her stummick ain't what it ought to be.

MRS. GIBBS:

All told, you won't get more'n three hours' sleep. Frank Gibbs, I don't know what's going to become of you. I do wish I could get you to go away someplace and take a rest. I think it would do you good.

MRS. WEBB:

Emileeee! Time to get up! Wally! Seven o'clock!

MRS. GIBBS:

I declare, you got to speak to George. Seems like something's come over him lately. He's no help to me at all. I can't even get him to cut me some wood.

DR. GIBBS:

Washing and drying his hands at the sink. MRS. GIBBS *is busy at the stove.*

Is he sassy to you?

MRS. GIBBS:

No. He just whines! All he thinks about is that baseball—George! Rebecca! You'll be late for school.

DR. GIBBS:

M-m-m . . .

MRS. GIBBS:

George!

DR. GIBBS:

George, look sharp!

GEORGE:

Offstage.

Yes, Pa!

DR. GIBBS:

As he goes off the stage.

Don't you hear your mother calling you? —I guess I'll go upstairs and get forty winks.

MRS. WEBB:

Walleee! Emileee! You'll be late for school! Walleee! You wash yourself good or I'll come up and do it myself.

REBECCA:

Offstage.

Ma! What dress shall I wear?

MRS. GIBBS:

Don't make a noise. Your father's been out all night and needs his sleep. I washed and ironed the blue gingham for you special.

REBECCA:

Ma, I hate that dress.

MRS. GIBBS:

Oh, hush-up-with-you.

REBECCA:

Every day I go to school dressed like a sick turkey.

MRS. GIBBS:

Now, Rebecca, you always look *very* nice.

REBECCA:

Mama, George's throwing soap at me.

MRS. GIBBS:

I'll come and slap the both of you, —that's what I'll do.

A factory whistle sounds.

The children dash in and take their places at the tables. Right, GEORGE, *about sixteen, and* REBECCA, *eleven. Left,* EMILY *and* WALLY, *same ages. They carry strapped schoolbooks.*

STAGE MANAGER:

We've got a factory in our town too—hear it? Makes blankets. Cartwrights own it and it brung 'em a fortune.

MRS. WEBB:

Children! Now I won't have it. Breakfast is just as good as any other meal and I won't have you gobbling like wolves. It'll stunt your growth, —that's a fact. Put away your book, Wally.

WALLY:

Aw, Ma! By ten o'clock I got to know all about Canada.

MRS. WEBB:

You know the rule's well as I do—no books at table. As for me, I'd rather have my children healthy than bright.

EMILY:

I'm both, Mama: you know I am. I'm the brightest girl in school for my age. I have a wonderful memory.

MRS. WEBB:

Eat your breakfast.

WALLY:

I'm bright, too, when I'm looking at my stamp collection.

MRS. GIBBS:

I'll speak to your father about it when he's rested. Seems to me twenty-five cents a week's enough for a boy your age. I declare I don't know how you spend it all.

GEORGE:

Aw, Ma, —I gotta lotta things to buy.

MRS. GIBBS:

Strawberry phosphates—that's what you spend it on.

GEORGE:

I don't see how Rebecca comes to have so much money. She has more'n a dollar.

REBECCA:

Spoon in mouth, dreamily.

I've been saving it up gradual.

MRS. GIBBS:

Well, dear, I think it's a good thing to spend some every now and then.

REBECCA:

Mama, do you know what I love most in the world—do you? —Money.

MRS. GIBBS:

Eat your breakfast.

THE CHILDREN:

Mama, there's first bell. —I gotta hurry. —I don't want any more. —I gotta hurry.

The children rise, seize their books and dash out through the

trellises. They meet, down center, and, chattering, walk to Main Street, then turn left.
The STAGE MANAGER *goes off, unobtrusively, right.*

MRS. WEBB:

Walk fast, but you don't have to run. Wally, pull up your pants at the knee. Stand up straight, Emily.

MRS. GIBBS:

Tell Miss Foster I send her my best congratulations—can you remember that?

REBECCA:

Yes, Ma.

MRS. GIBBS:

You look real nice, Rebecca. Pick up your feet.

ALL:

Good-by.

MRS. GIBBS *fills her apron with food for the chickens and comes down to the footlights.*

MRS. GIBBS:

Here, chick, chick, chick.
No, go away, you. Go away.
Here, chick, chick, chick.
What's the matter with *you?* Fight, fight, fight, —that's all you do.

Hm . . . *you* don't belong to me. Where'd you come from?

She shakes her apron.

Oh, don't be so scared. Nobody's going to hurt you.

MRS. WEBB *is sitting on the bench by her trellis, stringing beans.*

Good morning, Myrtle. How's your cold?

MRS. WEBB:

Well, I still get that tickling feeling in my throat. I told Charles I didn't know as I'd go to choir practice tonight. Wouldn't be any use.

MRS. GIBBS:

Have you tried singing over your voice?

MRS. WEBB:

Yes, but somehow I can't do that and stay on the key. While I'm resting myself I thought I'd string some of these beans.

MRS. GIBBS:

Rolling up her sleeves as she crosses the stage for a chat.

Let me help you. Beans have been good this year.

MRS. WEBB:

I've decided to put up forty quarts if it kills me. The children say they hate 'em, but I notice they're able to get 'em down all winter.

Pause. Brief sound of chickens cackling.

MRS. GIBBS:

Now, Myrtle. I've got to tell you something, because if I don't tell somebody I'll burst.

MRS. WEBB:

Why, Julia Gibbs!

MRS. GIBBS:

Here, give me some more of those beans. Myrtle, did one of those secondhand-furniture men from Boston come to see you last Friday?

MRS. WEBB:

No-o.

MRS. GIBBS:

Well, he called on me. First I thought he was a patient wantin' to see Dr. Gibbs. 'N he wormed his way into my parlor, and, Myrtle Webb, he offered me three hundred and fifty dollars for Grandmother Wentworth's highboy, as I'm sitting here!

MRS. WEBB:

Why, Julia Gibbs!

MRS. GIBBS:

He did! That old thing! Why, it was so big I didn't know where to put it and I almost give it to Cousin Hester Wilcox.

MRS. WEBB:

Well, you're going to take it, aren't you?

MRS. GIBBS:

I don't know.

MRS. WEBB:

You don't know—three hundred and fifty dollars! What's come over you?

MRS. GIBBS:

Well, if I could get the doctor to take the money and go away someplace on a real trip, I'd sell it like that. —Y'know, Myrtle, it's been the dream of my life to see Paris, France. —Oh, I don't know. It sounds crazy, I suppose, but for years I've been promising myself that if we ever had the chance—

MRS. WEBB:

How does the doctor feel about it?

MRS. GIBBS:

Well, I did beat about the bush a little and said that if I got a legacy—that's the way I put it—I'd make him take me somewhere.

MRS. WEBB:

M-m-m . . . What did he say?

MRS. GIBBS:

You know how he is. I haven't heard a serious word out of him since I've known him. No, he said, it might make him discontented with Grover's Corners to go traipsin' about Europe; better let well enough alone, he says. Every two years he makes a trip to the battlefields of the Civil War and that's enough treat for anybody, he says.

MRS. WEBB:

Well, Mr. Webb just *admires* the way Dr. Gibbs knows everything about the Civil War. Mr. Webb's a good mind to give up Napoleon and move over to the Civil War, only Dr. Gibbs being one of the greatest experts in the country just makes him despair.

MRS. GIBBS:

It's a fact! Dr. Gibbs is never so happy as when he's at Antietam or Gettysburg. The times I've walked over those hills, Myrtle, stopping at every bush and pacing it all out, like we were going to buy it.

MRS. WEBB:

Well, if that secondhand man's really serious about buyin' it, Julia, you sell it. And then you'll get to see Paris, all right. Just keep droppin' hints from time to time—that's how I got to see the Atlantic Ocean, y'know.

MRS. GIBBS:

Oh, I'm sorry I mentioned it. Only it seems to me that

once in your life before you die you ought to see a country where they don't talk in English and don't even want to.

The STAGE MANAGER *enters briskly from the right. He tips his hat to the ladies, who nod their heads.*

STAGE MANAGER:

Thank you, ladies. Thank you very much.

MRS. GIBBS *and* MRS. WEBB *gather up their things, return into their homes and disappear.*

Now we're going to skip a few hours.
But first we want a little more information about the town, kind of a scientific account, you might say.
So I've asked Professor Willard of our State University to sketch in a few details of our past history here.
Is Professor Willard here?

PROFESSOR WILLARD, *a rural savant, pince-nez on a wide satin ribbon, enters from the right with some notes in his hand.*

May I introduce Professor Willard of our State University.
A few brief notes, thank you, Professor—unfortunately our time is limited.

PROFESSOR WILLARD:

Grover's Corners . . . let me see . . . Grover's Corners lies on the old Pleistocene granite of the Appalachian range. I may say it's some of the oldest land in the world. We're very proud of that. A shelf of Devonian basalt crosses it with vestiges of Mesozoic shale, and some sandstone outcroppings; but that's all more recent: two hundred, three hundred million years old.

Some highly interesting fossils have been found . . . I may say: unique fossils . . . two miles out of town, in Silas Peckham's cow pasture. They can be seen at the museum in our University at any time—that is, at any reasonable time. Shall I read some of Professor Gruber's notes on the meteorological situation—mean precipitation, et cetera?

STAGE MANAGER:

Afraid we won't have time for that, Professor. We might have a few words on the history of man here.

PROFESSOR WILLARD:

Yes . . . anthropological data: Early Amerindian stock. Cotahatchee tribes . . . no evidence before the tenth century of this era . . . hm . . . now entirely disappeared . . . possible traces in three families. Migration toward the end of the seventeenth century of English brachiocephalic blue-eyed stock . . . for the most part. Since then some Slav and Mediterranean—

STAGE MANAGER:

And the population, Professor Willard?

PROFESSOR WILLARD:

Within the town limits: 2,640.

STAGE MANAGER:

Just a moment, Professor.

He whispers into the professor's ear.

PROFESSOR WILLARD:

Oh, yes, indeed? —The population, *at the moment*, is 2,642. The Postal District brings in 507 more, making a total of 3,149. —Mortality and birth rates: constant. —By MacPherson's gauge: 6.032.

STAGE MANAGER:

Thank you very much, Professor. We're all very much obliged to you, I'm sure.

PROFESSOR WILLARD:

Not at all, sir; not at all.

STAGE MANAGER:

This way, Professor, and thank you again.

Exit PROFESSOR WILLARD.

Now the political and social report: Editor Webb. —Oh, Mr. Webb?

MRS. WEBB *appears at her back door.*

MRS. WEBB:

He'll be here in a minute. . . . He just cut his hand while he was eatin' an apple.

STAGE MANAGER:

Thank you, Mrs. Webb.

MRS. WEBB:

Charles! Everybody's waitin'.

Exit MRS. WEBB.

STAGE MANAGER:

Mr. Webb is Publisher and Editor of the Grover's Corners *Sentinel*. That's our local paper, y'know.

MR. WEBB *enters from his house, pulling on his coat. His finger is bound in a handkerchief.*

MR. WEBB:

Well . . . I don't have to tell you that we're run here by a Board of Selectmen. —All males vote at the age of twenty-one. Women vote indirect. We're lower middle class: sprinkling of professional men . . . ten percent illiterate laborers. Politically, we're eighty-six percent Republicans; six percent Democrats; four percent Socialists; rest, indifferent.
Religiously, we're eighty-five percent Protestants; twelve percent Catholics; rest, indifferent.

STAGE MANAGER:

Have you any comments, Mr. Webb?

MR. WEBB:

Very ordinary town, if you ask me. Little better behaved than most. Probably a lot duller.
But our young people here seem to like it well enough. Ninety percent of 'em graduating from high school settle down right here to live—even when they've been away to college.

STAGE MANAGER:

Now, is there anyone in the audience who would like to ask Editor Webb anything about the town?

WOMAN IN THE BALCONY:

Is there much drinking in Grover's Corners?

MR. WEBB:

Well, ma'am, I wouldn't know what you'd call *much.* Satiddy nights the farmhands meet down in Ellery Greenough's stable and holler some. We've got one or two town drunks, but they're always having remorses every time an evangelist comes to town. No, ma'am, I'd say likker ain't a regular thing in the home here, except in the medicine chest. Right good for snake bite, y'know—always was.

BELLIGERENT MAN AT BACK OF AUDITORIUM:

Is there no one in town aware of—

STAGE MANAGER:

Come forward, will you, where we can all hear you—What were you saying?

BELLIGERENT MAN:

Is there no one in town aware of social injustice and industrial inequality?

MR. WEBB:

Oh, yes, everybody is—somethin' terrible. Seems like they spend most of their time talking about who's rich and who's poor.

BELLIGERENT MAN:

Then why don't they do something about it?

He withdraws without waiting for an answer.

MR. WEBB:

Well, I dunno. . . . I guess we're all hunting like everybody else for a way the diligent and sensible can rise to the top and the lazy and quarrelsome can sink to the bottom. But it ain't easy to find. Meanwhile, we do all we can to help those that can't help themselves and those that can we leave alone. —Are there any other questions?

LADY IN A BOX:

Oh, Mr. Webb? Mr. Webb, is there any culture or love of beauty in Grover's Corners?

MR. WEBB:

Well, ma'am, there ain't much—not in the sense you mean. Come to think of it, there's some girls that play the piano at High School Commencement; but they ain't happy about it. No, ma'am, there isn't much culture; but maybe this is the place to tell you that we've got a lot of pleasures of a kind here: we like the sun comin' up over the mountain in the morning, and we all notice a good deal about the birds. We pay a lot of attention to them. And we watch the change of the seasons; yes, everybody knows about them. But those other things—you're right, ma'am, —there ain't much. —*Robinson Crusoe* and the Bible; and Handel's "Largo," we all know that; and Whistler's "Mother"—those are just about as far as we go.

LADY IN A BOX:

So I thought. Thank you, Mr. Webb.

STAGE MANAGER:

Thank you, Mr. Webb.

MR. WEBB *retires.*

Now, we'll go back to the town. It's early afternoon. All 2,642 have had their dinners and all the dishes have been washed.

MR. WEBB, *having removed his coat, returns and starts pushing a lawn mower to and fro beside his house.*

There's an early-afternoon calm in our town: a buzzin' and a hummin' from the school buildings; only a few buggies on Main Street—the horses dozing at the hitching posts; you all remember what it's like. Doc Gibbs is in his office, tapping people and making them say "ah." Mr. Webb's cuttin' his lawn over there; one man in ten thinks it's a privilege to push his own lawn mower.

No, sir. It's later than I thought. There are the children coming home from school already.

Shrill girls' voices are heard, off left. EMILY *comes along Main Street, carrying some books. There are some signs that she is imagining herself to be a lady of startling elegance.*

EMILY:

I *can't,* Lois. I've got to go home and help my mother. I *promised.*

MR. WEBB:

Emily, walk simply. Who do you think you are today?

EMILY:

Papa, you're terrible. One minute you tell me to stand up straight and the next minute you call me names. I just don't listen to you.

She gives him an abrupt kiss.

MR. WEBB:

Golly, I never got a kiss from such a great lady before.

He goes out of sight. EMILY *leans over and picks some flowers by the gate of her house.*

GEORGE *comes careening down Main Street. He is throwing a ball up to dizzying heights, and waiting to catch it again. This sometimes requires his taking six steps backward. He bumps into an old lady invisible to us.*

GEORGE:

Excuse me, Mrs. Forrest.

STAGE MANAGER:

As Mrs. Forrest.

Go out and play in the fields, young man. You got no business playing baseball on Main Street.

GEORGE:

Awfully sorry, Mrs. Forrest. —Hello, Emily.

EMILY:

H'lo.

GEORGE:

You made a fine speech in class.

EMILY:

Well . . . I was really ready to make a speech about the Monroe Doctrine, but at the last minute Miss Corcoran made me talk about the Louisiana Purchase instead. I worked an awful long time on both of them.

GEORGE:

Gee, it's funny, Emily. From my window up there I can just see your head nights when you're doing your homework over in your room.

EMILY:

Why, can you?

GEORGE:

You certainly do stick to it, Emily. I don't see how you can sit still that long. I guess you like school.

EMILY:

Well, I always feel it's something you have to go through.

GEORGE:

Yeah.

EMILY:

I don't mind it really. It passes the time.

GEORGE:

Yeah. —Emily, what do you think? We might work out a

kinda telegraph from your window to mine; and once in a while you could give me a kinda hint or two about one of those algebra problems. I don't mean the answers, Emily, of course not . . . just some little hint . . .

EMILY:

Oh, I think *hints* are allowed. —So—ah—if you get stuck, George, you whistle to me; and I'll give you some hints.

GEORGE:

Emily, you're just naturally bright, I guess.

EMILY:

I figure that it's just the way a person's born.

GEORGE:

Yeah. But, you see, I want to be a farmer, and my Uncle Luke says whenever I'm ready I can come over and work on his farm and if I'm any good I can just gradually have it.

EMILY:

You mean the house and everything?

Enter MRS. WEBB *with a large bowl and sits on the bench by her trellis.*

GEORGE:

Yeah. Well, thanks. . . . I better be getting out to the baseball field. Thanks for the talk, Emily. —Good afternoon, Mrs. Webb.

MRS. WEBB:

Good afternoon, George.

GEORGE:

So long, Emily.

EMILY:

So long, George.

MRS. WEBB:

Emily, come and help me string these beans for the winter.
George Gibbs let himself have a real conversation, didn't he? Why, he's growing up. How old would George be?

EMILY:

I don't know.

MRS. WEBB:

Let's see. He must be almost sixteen.

EMILY:

Mama, I made a speech in class today and I was very good.

MRS. WEBB:

You must recite it to your father at supper. What was it about?

EMILY:

The Louisiana Purchase. It was like silk off a spool. I'm

going to make speeches all my life. —Mama, are these big enough?

MRS. WEBB:

Try and get them a little bigger if you can.

EMILY:

Mama, will you answer me a question, serious?

MRS. WEBB:

Seriously, dear—not serious.

EMILY:

Seriously, —will you?

MRS. WEBB:

Of course, I will.

EMILY:

Mama, am I good looking?

MRS. WEBB:

Yes, of course you are. All my children have got good features; I'd be ashamed if they hadn't.

EMILY:

Oh, Mama, that's not what I mean. What I mean is: am I *pretty?*

MRS. WEBB:

I've already told you, yes. Now that's enough of that. You have a nice young pretty face. I never heard of such foolishness.

EMILY:

Oh, Mama, you never tell us the truth about anything.

MRS. WEBB:

I *am* telling you the truth.

EMILY:

Mama, were *you* pretty?

MRS. WEBB:

Yes, I was, if I do say it. I was the prettiest girl in town next to Mamie Cartwright.

EMILY:

But, Mama, you've got to say *some*thing about me. Am I pretty enough . . . to get anybody . . . to get people interested in me?

MRS. WEBB:

Emily, you make me tired. Now stop it. You're pretty enough for all normal purposes. —Come along now and bring that bowl with you.

EMILY:

Oh, Mama, you're no help at all.

STAGE MANAGER:

Thank you. Thank you! That'll do. We'll have to interrupt again here. Thank you, Mrs. Webb; thank you, Emily.

MRS. WEBB *and* EMILY *withdraw.*

There are some more things we want to explore about this town.

He comes to the center of the stage. During the following speech the lights gradually dim to darkness, leaving only a spot on him.

I think this is a good time to tell you that the Cartwright interests have just begun building a new bank in Grover's Corners—had to go to Vermont for the marble, sorry to say. And they've asked a friend of mine what they should put in the cornerstone for people to dig up . . . a thousand years from now. . . . Of course, they've put in a copy of the *New York Times* and a copy of Mr. Webb's *Sentinel*. . . . We're kind of interested in this because some scientific fellas have found a way of painting all that reading matter with a glue—a silicate glue—that'll make it keep a thousand—two thousand years.

We're putting in a Bible . . . and the Constitution of the United States—and a copy of William Shakespeare's plays. What do you say, folks? What do you think?

Y'know—Babylon once had two million people in it, and all we know about 'em is the names of the kings and some copies of wheat contracts . . . and contracts for the sale of slaves. Yet every night all those families sat down to supper, and the father came home from his work, and the smoke went up the chimney, —same as here. And even in Greece and Rome, all we know about the *real* life of the

people is what we can piece together out of the joking poems and the comedies they wrote for the theatre back then.
So I'm going to have a copy of this play put in the cornerstone and the people a thousand years from now'll know a few simple facts about us—more than the Treaty of Versailles and the Lindbergh flight.
See what I mean?
So—people a thousand years from now—this is the way we were in the provinces north of New York at the beginning of the twentieth century. —This is the way we were: in our growing up and in our marrying and in our living and in our dying.

A choir partially concealed in the orchestra pit has begun singing "Blessed Be the Tie That Binds."

SIMON STIMSON *stands directing them.*

Two ladders have been pushed onto the stage; they serve as indication of the second story in the Gibbs and Webb houses. GEORGE *and* EMILY *mount them, and apply themselves to their schoolwork.*

DR. GIBBS *has entered and is seated in his kitchen reading.*

Well! —good deal of time's gone by. It's evening.
You can hear choir practice going on in the Congregational Church.
The children are at home doing their schoolwork.
The day's running down like a tired clock.

SIMON STIMSON:

Now look here, everybody. Music come into the world to give pleasure. —Softer! Softer! Get it out of your heads that music's only good when it's loud. You leave loudness to the Methodists. You couldn't beat 'em, even if you wanted to. Now again. Tenors!

GEORGE:

Hssst! Emily!

EMILY:

Hello.

GEORGE:

Hello!

EMILY:

I can't work at all. The moonlight's so *terrible*.

GEORGE:

Emily, did you get the third problem?

EMILY:

Which?

GEORGE:

The *third?*

EMILY:

Why, yes, George—that's the easiest of them all.

GEORGE:

I don't see it. Emily, can you give me a hint?

EMILY:

I'll tell you one thing: the answer's in yards.

GEORGE:

!!! In yards? How do you mean?

EMILY:

In *square* yards.

GEORGE:

Oh . . . in square yards.

EMILY:

Yes, George, don't you see?

GEORGE:

Yeah.

EMILY:

In square yards of *wallpaper*.

GEORGE:

Wallpaper—oh, I see. Thanks a lot, Emily.

EMILY:

You're welcome. My, isn't the moonlight *terrible?* And choir practice going on. —I think if you hold your breath you can hear the train all the way to Contoocook. Hear it?

GEORGE:

M-m-m— What do you know!

EMILY:

Well, I guess I better go back and try to work.

GEORGE:

Good night, Emily. And thanks.

EMILY:

Good night, George.

SIMON STIMSON:

Before I forget it: how many of you will be able to come in Tuesday afternoon and sing at Fred Hersey's wedding? —show your hands. That'll be fine; that'll be right nice. We'll do the same music we did for Jane Trowbridge's last month.
—Now we'll do "Art Thou Weary; Art Thou Languid?" It's a question, ladies and gentlemen, make it talk. Ready.

DR. GIBBS:

Oh, George, can you come down a minute?

GEORGE:

Yes, Pa.

He descends the ladder.

DR. GIBBS:

Make yourself comfortable, George; I'll only keep you a minute.
George, how old are you?

GEORGE:

I? I'm sixteen, almost seventeen.

DR. GIBBS:

What do you want to do after school's over?

GEORGE:

Why, you know, Pa. I want to be a farmer on Uncle Luke's farm.

DR. GIBBS:

You'll be willing, will you, to get up early and milk and feed the stock . . . and you'll be able to hoe and hay all day?

GEORGE:

Sure, I will. What are you . . . what do you mean, Pa?

DR. GIBBS:

Well, George, while I was in my office today I heard a funny sound . . . and what do you think it was? It was your mother chopping wood. There you see your mother—getting up early; cooking meals all day long; washing and ironing—and still she has to go out in the backyard and chop wood. I suppose she just got tired of asking you. She just gave up and decided it was easier to do it herself. And you eat her meals, and put on the clothes she keeps nice for you, and you run off and play baseball, —like she's some hired girl we keep around the house but that we don't like very much.

GEORGE *snuffles.*

Well, I knew all I had to do was call your attention to it. Here's a handkerchief, son. George, I've decided to raise your spending money twenty-five cents a week. Not, of course, for chopping wood for your mother, because that's a present you give her, but because you're getting older—and I imagine there are lots of things you must find to do with it.

GEORGE:

Thanks, Pa.

DR. GIBBS:

Let's see—tomorrow's your payday. You can count on it— Hmm. Probably Rebecca'll feel she ought to have some more too. Wonder what could have happened to your mother. Choir practice never was as late as this before.

GEORGE:

It's only half past eight, Pa.

DR. GIBBS:

I don't know why she's in that old choir. She hasn't any

more voice than an old crow. . . . Traipsin' around the streets at this hour of the night. . . . Just about time you retired, don't you think?

GEORGE:

Yes, Pa.

GEORGE *mounts to his place on the ladder.*

Laughter and good-nights can be heard on stage left and presently MRS. GIBBS, MRS. SOAMES, *and* MRS. WEBB *come down Main Street. When they arrive at the corner of the stage they stop.*

MRS. SOAMES:

Good night, Martha. Good night, Mr. Foster.

MRS. WEBB:

I'll tell Mr. Webb; I *know* he'll want to put it in the paper.

MRS. GIBBS:

My, it's late!

MRS. SOAMES:

Good night, Irma.

MRS. GIBBS:

Real nice choir practice, wa'n't it? Myrtle Webb! Look at that moon, will you! Tsk-tsk-tsk. Potato weather, for sure.

They are silent a moment, gazing up at the moon.

MRS. SOAMES:

Naturally I didn't want to say a word about it in front of those others, but now we're alone—really, it's the worst scandal that ever was in this town.

MRS. GIBBS:

What?

MRS. SOAMES:

Simon Stimson!

MRS. GIBBS:

Now, Louella!

MRS. SOAMES:

But, Julia! To have the organist of a church *drink* and *drunk* year after year. You know he was drunk tonight.

MRS. GIBBS:

Now, Louella! We all know about Mr. Stimson, and we all know about the troubles he's been through, and Dr. Ferguson knows too, and if Dr. Ferguson keeps him on there in his job the only thing the rest of us can do is just not to notice it.

MRS. SOAMES:

Not to notice it! But it's getting worse.

MRS. WEBB:

No, it isn't, Louella. It's getting better. I've been in that choir twice as long as you have. It doesn't happen anywhere near so often. . . . My, I hate to go to bed on a night like this. —I better hurry. Those children'll be sitting up till all hours. Good night, Louella.

They all exchange good-nights. She hurries downstage, enters her house and disappears.

MRS. GIBBS:

Can you get home safe, Louella?

MRS. SOAMES:

It's as bright as day. I can see Mr. Soames scowling at the window now. You'd think we'd been to a dance the way the menfolk carry on.

More good-nights. MRS. GIBBS *arrives at her home and passes through the trellis into the kitchen.*

MRS. GIBBS:

Well, we had a real good time.

DR. GIBBS:

You're late enough.

MRS. GIBBS:

Why, Frank, it ain't any later'n usual.

DR. GIBBS:

And you stopping at the corner to gossip with a lot of hens.

MRS. GIBBS:

Now, Frank, don't be grouchy. Come out and smell the heliotrope in the moonlight.

They stroll out arm in arm along the footlights.

Isn't that wonderful? What did you do all the time I was away?

DR. GIBBS:

Oh, I read—as usual. What were the girls gossiping about tonight?

MRS. GIBBS:

Well, believe me, Frank—there is something to gossip about.

DR. GIBBS:

Hmm! Simon Stimson far gone, was he?

MRS. GIBBS:

Worst I've ever seen him. How'll that end, Frank? Dr. Ferguson can't forgive him forever.

DR. GIBBS:

I guess I know more about Simon Stimson's affairs than anybody in this town. Some people ain't made for small-town life. I don't know how that'll end; but there's nothing we can do but just leave it alone. Come, get in.

MRS. GIBBS:

No, not yet. . . . Frank, I'm worried about you.

DR. GIBBS:

What are you worried about?

MRS. GIBBS:

I think it's my duty to make plans for you to get a real rest and change. And if I get that legacy, well, I'm going to insist on it.

DR. GIBBS:

Now, Julia, there's no sense in going over that again.

MRS. GIBBS:

Frank, you're just *unreasonable!*

DR. GIBBS:

Starting into the house.

Come on, Julia, it's getting late. First thing you know you'll catch cold. I gave George a piece of my mind tonight. I reckon you'll have your wood chopped for a while anyway.

MRS. GIBBS *picks up string from floor.*

No, no, start getting upstairs.

MRS. GIBBS:

Oh, dear. There's always so many things to pick up, seems like.

You know, Frank, Mrs. Fairchild always locks her front door every night. All those people up that part of town do.

DR. GIBBS:

Blowing out the lamp.

They're all getting citified, that's the trouble with them. They haven't got nothing fit to burgle and everybody knows it.

They disappear.

REBECCA *climbs up the ladder beside* GEORGE.

GEORGE:

Get out, Rebecca. There's only room for one at this window. You're always spoiling everything.

REBECCA:

Well, let me look just a minute.

GEORGE:

Use your own window.

REBECCA:

I did, but there's no moon there. . . . George, do you know what I think, do you? I think maybe the moon's getting nearer and nearer and there'll be a big 'splosion.

GEORGE:

Rebecca, you don't know anything. If the moon were getting nearer, the guys that sit up all night with telescopes would see it first and they'd tell about it, and it'd be in all the newspapers.

REBECCA:

George, is the moon shining on South America, Canada, and half the whole world?

GEORGE:

Well—prob'ly is.

The STAGE MANAGER *strolls on.*

Pause. The sound of crickets is heard.

STAGE MANAGER:

Nine thirty. Most of the lights are out. No, there's Constable Warren trying a few doors on Main Street. And here comes Editor Webb, after putting his newspaper to bed.

MR. WARREN, *an elderly policeman, comes along Main Street from the right,* MR. WEBB *from the left.*

MR. WEBB:

Good evening, Bill.

CONSTABLE WARREN:

Evenin', Mr. Webb.

MR. WEBB:

Quite a moon!

CONSTABLE WARREN:

Yepp.

MR. WEBB:

All quiet tonight?

CONSTABLE WARREN:

Simon Stimson is rollin' around a little. Just saw his wife movin' out to hunt for him so I looked the other way—there he is now.

SIMON STIMSON *comes down Main Street from the left, only a trace of unsteadiness in his walk.*

MR. WEBB:

Good evening, Simon. . . . Town seems to have settled down for the night pretty well. . . .

SIMON STIMSON *comes up to him and pauses a moment and stares at him, swaying slightly.*

Good evening. . . . Yes, most of the town's settled down for the night, Simon. . . . I guess we better do the same. Can I walk along a ways with you?

SIMON STIMSON *continues on his way without a word and disappears at the right.*

Good night.

CONSTABLE WARREN:

I don't know how that's going to end, Mr. Webb.

MR. WEBB:

Well, he's seen a peck of trouble, one thing after another. . . . Oh, Bill . . . if you see my boy smoking cigarettes, just give him a word, will you? He thinks a lot of you, Bill.

CONSTABLE WARREN:

I don't think he smokes no cigarettes, Mr. Webb. Leastways, not more'n two or three a year.

MR. WEBB:

Hm . . . I hope not. —Well, good night, Bill.

CONSTABLE WARREN:

Good night, Mr. Webb.
Exit.

MR. WEBB:

Who's that up there? Is that you, Myrtle?

EMILY:

No, it's me, Papa.

MR. WEBB:

Why aren't you in bed?

EMILY:

I don't know. I just can't sleep yet, Papa. The moonlight's so *won*-derful. And the smell of Mrs. Gibbs' heliotrope. Can you smell it?

MR. WEBB:

Hm . . . Yes. Haven't any troubles on your mind, have you, Emily?

EMILY:

Troubles, Papa? *No.*

MR. WEBB:

Well, enjoy yourself, but don't let your mother catch you. Good night, Emily.

EMILY:

Good night, Papa.

MR. WEBB *crosses into the house, whistling "Blessed Be the Tie That Binds," and disappears.*

REBECCA:

I never told you about that letter Jane Crofut got from her minister when she was sick. He wrote Jane a letter and on the envelope the address was like this: It said: Jane Crofut; the Crofut Farm; Grover's Corners; Sutton County; New Hampshire; United States of America.

GEORGE:

What's funny about that?

REBECCA:

But listen, it's not finished: the United States of America; Continent of North America; Western Hemisphere; the Earth; the Solar System; the Universe; the Mind of God—that's what it said on the envelope.

GEORGE:

What do you know!

REBECCA:

And the postman brought it just the same.

GEORGE:

What do you know!

STAGE MANAGER:

That's the end of the First Act, friends. You can go and smoke now, those that smoke.

Act Two

The tables and chairs of the two kitchens are still on the stage.
The ladders and the small bench have been withdrawn.
The STAGE MANAGER *has been at his accustomed place watching the audience return to its seats.*

STAGE MANAGER:

Three years have gone by.
Yes, the sun's come up over a thousand times.
Summers and winters have cracked the mountains a little bit more and the rains have brought down some of the dirt.
Some babies that weren't even born before have begun talking regular sentences already; and a number of people who thought they were right young and spry have noticed that they can't bound up a flight of stairs like they used to, without their heart fluttering a little.
All that can happen in a thousand days.
Nature's been pushing and contriving in other ways, too: a number of young people fell in love and got married.
Yes, the mountain got bit away a few fractions of an inch; millions of gallons of water went by the mill; and here and there a new home was set up under a roof.
Almost everybody in the world gets married—you know what I mean? In our town there aren't hardly any excep-

tions. Most everybody in the world climbs into their graves married.
The First Act was called the Daily Life. This act is called Love and Marriage. There's another act coming after this: I reckon you can guess what that's about.
So:
It's three years later. It's 1904.
It's July 7th, just after High School Commencement.
That's the time most of our young people jump up and get married.
Soon as they've passed their last examinations in solid geometry and Cicero's Orations, looks like they suddenly feel themselves fit to be married.
It's early morning. Only this time it's been raining. It's been pouring and thundering.
Mrs. Gibbs' garden, and Mrs. Webb's here: drenched.
All those bean poles and peavines: drenched.
All yesterday over there on Main Street, the rain looked like curtains being blown along.
Hm . . . it may begin again any minute.
There! You can hear the 5:45 for Boston.

MRS. GIBBS *and* MRS. WEBB *enter their kitchens and start the day as in the First Act.*

And there's Mrs. Gibbs and Mrs. Webb come down to make breakfast, just as though it were an ordinary day. I don't have to point out to the women in my audience that those ladies they see before them, both of those ladies cooked three meals a day—one of 'em for twenty years, the other for forty—and no summer vacation. They brought up two children apiece, washed, cleaned the house, —and *never a nervous breakdown*.

It's like what one of those Middle West poets said: You've got to love life to have life, and you've got to have life to love life. . . . It's what they call a vicious circle.

HOWIE NEWSOME:

Offstage left.

Giddap, Bessie!

STAGE MANAGER:

Here comes Howie Newsome delivering the milk. And there's Si Crowell delivering the papers like his brother before him.

SI CROWELL *has entered, hurling imaginary newspapers into doorways;* HOWIE NEWSOME *has come along Main Street with Bessie.*

SI CROWELL:

Morning, Howie.

HOWIE NEWSOME:

Morning, Si. —Anything in the papers I ought to know?

SI CROWELL:

Nothing much, except we're losing about the best baseball pitcher Grover's Corners ever had—George Gibbs.

HOWIE NEWSOME:

Reckon he is.

SI CROWELL:

He could hit and run bases, too.

HOWIE NEWSOME:

Yep. Mighty fine ball player. —Whoa! Bessie! I guess I can stop and talk if I've a mind to!

SI CROWELL:

I don't see how he could give up a thing like that just to get married. Would you, Howie?

HOWIE NEWSOME:

Can't tell, Si. Never had no talent that way.

CONSTABLE WARREN *enters. They exchange good-mornings.*

You're up early, Bill.

CONSTABLE WARREN:

Seein' if there's anything I can do to prevent a flood. River's been risin' all night.

HOWIE NEWSOME:

Si Crowell's all worked up here about George Gibbs' retiring from baseball.

CONSTABLE WARREN:

Yes, sir; that's the way it goes. Back in '84 we had a player, Si—even George Gibbs couldn't touch him. Name of Hank Todd. Went down to Maine and become a parson. Wonderful ball player. —Howie, how does the weather look to you?

HOWIE NEWSOME:

Oh, 'tain't bad. Think maybe it'll clear up for good.

CONSTABLE WARREN *and* SI CROWELL *continue on their way.*

HOWIE NEWSOME *brings the milk first to Mrs. Gibbs' house. She meets him by the trellis.*

MRS. GIBBS:

Good morning, Howie. Do you think it's going to rain again?

HOWIE NEWSOME:

Morning, Mrs. Gibbs. It rained so heavy, I think maybe it'll clear up.

MRS. GIBBS:

Certainly hope it will.

HOWIE NEWSOME:

How much did you want today?

MRS. GIBBS:

I'm going to have a houseful of relations, Howie. Looks to me like I'll need three-a-milk and two-a-cream.

HOWIE NEWSOME:

My wife says to tell you we both hope they'll be very happy, Mrs. Gibbs. Know they *will*.

MRS. GIBBS:

Thanks a lot, Howie. Tell your wife I hope she gits there to the wedding.

HOWIE NEWSOME:

Yes, she'll be there; she'll be there if she kin.

HOWIE NEWSOME *crosses to Mrs. Webb's house.*

Morning, Mrs. Webb.

MRS. WEBB:

Oh, good morning, Mr. Newsome. I told you four quarts of milk, but I hope you can spare me another.

HOWIE NEWSOME:

Yes'm . . . and the two of cream.

MRS. WEBB:

Will it start raining again, Mr. Newsome?

HOWIE NEWSOME:

Well. Just sayin' to Mrs. Gibbs as how it may lighten up. Mrs. Newsome told me to tell you how we hope they'll both be very happy, Mrs. Webb. Know they *will.*

MRS. WEBB:

Thank you, and thank Mrs. Newsome and we're counting on seeing you at the wedding.

HOWIE NEWSOME:

Yes, Mrs. Webb. We hope to git there. Couldn't miss that. Come on, Bessie.

Exit HOWIE NEWSOME.

DR. GIBBS *descends in shirt sleeves, and sits down at his breakfast table.*

DR. GIBBS:

Well, Ma, the day has come. You're losin' one of your chicks.

MRS. GIBBS:

Frank Gibbs, don't you say another word. I feel like crying every minute. Sit down and drink your coffee.

DR. GIBBS:

The groom's up shaving himself—only there ain't an awful lot to shave. Whistling and singing, like he's glad to leave us. —Every now and then he says "I do" to the mirror, but it don't sound convincing to me.

MRS. GIBBS:

I declare, Frank, I don't know how he'll get along. I've arranged his clothes and seen to it he's put warm things on—Frank! they're too *young*. Emily won't think of such things. He'll catch his death of cold within a week.

DR. GIBBS:

I was remembering my wedding morning, Julia.

MRS. GIBBS:

Now don't start that, Frank Gibbs.

DR. GIBBS:

I was the scaredest young fella in the State of New Hampshire. I thought I'd made a mistake for sure. And when I saw you comin' down that aisle I thought you were the prettiest girl I'd even seen, but the only trouble was that I'd never seen you before. There I was in the Congregational Church marryin' a total stranger.

MRS. GIBBS:

And how do you think I felt! —Frank, weddings are perfectly awful things. Farces, —that's what they are!

She puts a plate before him.

Here, I've made something for you.

DR. GIBBS:

Why, Julia Hersey—French toast!

MRS. GIBBS:

'Tain't hard to make and I had to do *some*thing.

Pause. DR. GIBBS *pours on the syrup.*

DR. GIBBS:

How'd you sleep last night, Julia?

MRS. GIBBS:

Well, I heard a lot of the hours struck off.

DR. GIBBS:

Ye-e-s! I get a shock every time I think of George setting out to be a family man—that great gangling thing! —I tell you, Julia, there's nothing so terrifying in the world as a *son*. The relation of father and son is the darndest, awkwardest—

MRS. GIBBS:

Well, mother and daughter's no picnic, let me tell you.

DR. GIBBS:

They'll have a lot of troubles, I suppose, but that's none of our business. Everybody has a right to their own troubles.

MRS. GIBBS:

At the table, drinking her coffee, meditatively.

Yes . . . people are meant to go through life two by two. 'Tain't natural to be lonesome.

Pause. DR. GIBBS *starts laughing.*

DR. GIBBS:

Julia, do you know one of the things I was scared of when I married you?

MRS. GIBBS:

Oh, go along with you!

DR. GIBBS:

I was afraid we wouldn't have material for conversation more'n'd last us a few weeks.

Both laugh.

I was afraid we'd run out and eat our meals in silence, that's a fact. —Well, you and I been conversing for twenty years now without any noticeable barren spells.

MRS. GIBBS:

Well, —good weather, bad weather—'tain't very choice, but I always find something to say.

She goes to the foot of the stairs.

Did you hear Rebecca stirring around upstairs?

DR. GIBBS:

No. Only day of the year Rebecca hasn't been managing everybody's business up there. She's hiding in her room. —I got the impression she's crying.

MRS. GIBBS:

Lord's sakes! —This has got to stop. —Rebecca! Rebecca! Come and get your breakfast.

GEORGE *comes rattling down the stairs, very brisk.*

GEORGE:

Good morning, everybody. Only five more hours to live.

Makes the gesture of cutting his throat, and a loud "k-k-k," and starts through the trellis.

MRS. GIBBS:

George Gibbs, where are you going?

GEORGE:

Just stepping across the grass to see my girl.

MRS. GIBBS:

Now, George! You put on your overshoes. It's raining torrents. You don't go out of this house without you're prepared for it.

GEORGE:

Aw, Ma. It's just a *step!*

MRS. GIBBS:

George! You'll catch your death of cold and cough all through the service.

DR. GIBBS:

George, do as your mother tells you!

DR. GIBBS *goes upstairs.*

GEORGE *returns reluctantly to the kitchen and pantomimes putting on overshoes.*

MRS. GIBBS:

From tomorrow on you can kill yourself in all weathers, but while you're in my house you'll live wisely, thank you. —Maybe Mrs. Webb isn't used to callers at seven in the morning. —Here, take a cup of coffee first.

GEORGE:

Be back in a minute.

He crosses the stage, leaping over the puddles.

Good morning, Mother Webb.

MRS. WEBB:

Goodness! You frightened me! —Now, George, you can come in a minute out of the wet, but you know I can't ask you in.

GEORGE:

Why not—?

MRS. WEBB:

George, you know's well as I do: the groom can't see his bride on his wedding day, not until he sees her in church.

GEORGE:

Aw! —that's just a superstition. —Good morning, Mr. Webb.

Enter MR. WEBB.

MR. WEBB:

Good morning, George.

GEORGE:

Mr. Webb, you don't believe in that superstition, do you?

MR. WEBB:

There's a lot of common sense in some superstitions, George.

He sits at the table, facing right.

MRS. WEBB:

Millions have folla'd it, George, and you don't want to be the first to fly in the face of custom.

GEORGE:

How is Emily?

MRS. WEBB:

She hasn't waked up yet. I haven't heard a sound out of her.

GEORGE:

Emily's *asleep!!!*

MRS. WEBB:

No wonder! We were up 'til all hours, sewing and packing. Now I'll tell you what I'll do; you set down here a minute with Mr. Webb and drink this cup of coffee; and I'll go upstairs and see she doesn't come down and surprise you. There's some bacon, too; but don't be long about it.

Exit MRS. WEBB.

Embarrassed silence.

MR. WEBB *dunks doughnuts in his coffee.*

More silence.

MR. WEBB:

Suddenly and loudly.

Well, George, how are you?

GEORGE:

Startled, choking over his coffee.

Oh, fine, I'm fine.

Pause.

Mr. Webb, what sense could there be in a superstition like that?

MR. WEBB:

Well, you see, —on her wedding morning a girl's head's apt to be full of . . . clothes and one thing and another. Don't you think that's probably it?

GEORGE:

Ye-e-s. I never thought of that.

MR. WEBB:

A girl's apt to be a mite nervous on her wedding day.
Pause.

GEORGE:

I wish a fellow could get married without all that marching up and down.

MR. WEBB:

Every man that's ever lived has felt that way about it, George; but it hasn't been any use. It's the womenfolk who've built up weddings, my boy. For a while now the women have it all their own. A man looks pretty small at a wedding, George. All those good women standing shoulder to shoulder making sure that the knot's tied in a mighty public way.

GEORGE:

But . . . you *believe* in it, don't you, Mr. Webb?

MR. WEBB:

With alacrity.
Oh, yes; *oh, yes*. Don't you misunderstand me, my boy. Marriage is a wonderful thing, —wonderful thing. And don't you forget that, George.

GEORGE:

No, sir. —Mr. Webb, how old were you when you got married?

MR. WEBB:

Well, you see: I'd been to college and I'd taken a little time to get settled. But Mrs. Webb—she wasn't much older than what Emily is. Oh, age hasn't much to do with it, George—not compared with . . . uh . . . other things.

GEORGE:

What were you going to say, Mr. Webb?

MR. WEBB:

Oh, I don't know. —Was I going to say something?

Pause.

George, I was thinking the other night of some advice my father gave me when I got married. Charles, he said, Charles, start out early showing who's boss, he said. Best thing to do is to give an order, even if it don't make sense; just so she'll learn to obey. And he said: if anything about your wife irritates you—her conversation, or anything—just get up and leave the house. That'll make it clear to her, he said. And, oh, yes! he said never, *never* let your wife know how much money you have, never.

GEORGE:

Well, Mr. Webb . . . I don't think I could . . .

MR. WEBB:

So I took the opposite of my father's advice and I've been

happy ever since. And let that be a lesson to you, George, never to ask advice on personal matters. —George, are you going to raise chickens on your farm?

GEORGE:

What?

MR. WEBB:

Are you going to raise chickens on your farm?

GEORGE:

Uncle Luke's never been much interested, but I thought—

MR. WEBB:

A book came into my office the other day, George, on the Philo System of raising chickens. I want you to read it. I'm thinking of beginning in a small way in the backyard, and I'm going to put an incubator in the cellar—

Enter MRS. WEBB.

MRS. WEBB:

Charles, are you talking about that old incubator again? I thought you two'd be talking about things worthwhile.

MR. WEBB:

Bitingly.

Well, Myrtle, if you want to give the boy some good advice, I'll go upstairs and leave you alone with him.

MRS. WEBB:

Pulling GEORGE *up.*

George, Emily's got to come downstairs and eat her breakfast. She sends you her love but she doesn't want to lay eyes on you. Good-by.

GEORGE:

Good-by.

GEORGE *crosses the stage to his own home, bewildered and crestfallen. He slowly dodges a puddle and disappears into his house.*

MR. WEBB:

Myrtle, I guess you don't know about that older superstition.

MRS. WEBB:

What do you mean, Charles?

MR. WEBB:

Since the cavemen: no bridegroom should see his father-in-law on the day of the wedding, or near it. Now remember that.

Both leave the stage.

STAGE MANAGER:

Thank you very much, Mr. and Mrs. Webb. —Now I have to interrupt again here. You see, we want to know how all this began—this wedding, this plan to spend a life-

time together. I'm awfully interested in how big things like that begin.
You know how it is: you're twenty-one or twenty-two and you make some decisions; then whisssh! you're seventy: you've been a lawyer for fifty years, and that white-haired lady at your side has eaten over fifty thousand meals with you.
How do such things begin?
George and Emily are going to show you now the conversation they had when they first knew that . . . that . . . as the saying goes . . . they were meant for one another.
But before they do it I want you to try and remember what it was like to have been very young.
And particularly the days when you were first in love; when you were like a person sleepwalking, and you didn't quite see the street you were in, and didn't quite hear everything that was said to you.
You're just a little bit crazy. Will you remember that, please?
Now they'll be coming out of high school at three o'clock. George has just been elected President of the Junior Class, and as it's June, that means he'll be President of the Senior Class all next year. And Emily's just been elected Secretary and Treasurer. I don't have to tell you how important that is.

He places a board across the backs of two chairs, which he takes from those at the Gibbs family's table. He brings two high stools from the wings and places them behind the board. Persons sitting on the stools will be facing the audience. This is the counter of Mr. Morgan's drugstore.
The sounds of young people's voices are heard off left.

Yepp, —there they are coming down Main Street now.

EMILY, *carrying an armful of imaginary schoolbooks, comes along Main Street from the left.*

EMILY:

I can't, Louise. I've got to go home. Good-by. Oh, Ernestine! Ernestine! Can you come over tonight and do Latin? Isn't that Cicero the worst thing—! Tell your mother you *have* to. G'by. G'by, Helen. G'by, Fred.

GEORGE, *also carrying books, catches up with her.*

GEORGE:

Can I carry your books home for you, Emily?

EMILY:

Coolly.

Why . . . uh . . . Thank you. It isn't far.

She gives them to him.

GEORGE:

Excuse me a minute, Emily. —Say, Bob, if I'm a little late, start practice anyway. And give Herb some long high ones.

EMILY:

Good-by, Lizzy.

GEORGE:

Good-by, Lizzy. —I'm awfully glad you were elected, too, Emily.

EMILY:

Thank you.

They have been standing on Main Street, almost against the back wall. They take the first steps toward the audience when GEORGE *stops and speaks.*

GEORGE:

Emily, why are you mad at me?

EMILY:

I'm not mad at you.

GEORGE:

You've been treating me so funny lately.

EMILY:

Well, since you ask me, I might as well say it right out, George—

She catches sight of a teacher passing.

Good-by, Miss Corcoran.

GEORGE:

Good-by, Miss Corcoran. —Wha—what is it?

EMILY:

Not scoldingly; finding it difficult to say.

I don't like the whole change that's come over you in the last year. I'm sorry if that hurts your feelings, but I've got to—tell the truth and shame the devil.

GEORGE:

A *change*? —Wha—what do you mean?

EMILY:

Well, up to a year ago I used to like you a lot. And I used to watch you as you did everything . . . because we'd been friends so long . . . and then you began spending all your time at *baseball* . . . and you never stopped to speak to anybody anymore. Not even to your own family you didn't . . . and, George, it's a fact, you've got awful conceited and stuck-up, and all the girls say so. They may not say so to your face, but that's what they say about you behind your back, and it hurts me to hear them say it, but I've got to agree with them a little. I'm sorry if it hurts your feelings . . . but I can't be sorry I said it.

GEORGE:

I . . . I'm glad you said it, Emily. I never thought that such a thing was happening to me. I guess it's hard for a fella not to have faults creep into his character.

They take a step or two in silence, then stand still in misery.

EMILY:

I always expect a man to be perfect and I think he should be.

GEORGE:

Oh . . . I don't think it's possible to be perfect, Emily.

EMILY:

Well, my *father* is, and as far as I can see *your* father is. There's no reason on earth why you shouldn't be, too.

GEORGE:

Well, I feel it's the other way round. That men aren't naturally good; but girls are.

EMILY:

Well, you might as well know right now that I'm not perfect. It's not as easy for a girl to be perfect as a man, because we girls are more—more—nervous. —Now I'm sorry I said all that about you. I don't know what made me say it.

GEORGE:

Emily—

EMILY:

Now I can see it's not the truth at all. And I suddenly feel that it isn't important, anyway.

GEORGE:

Emily . . . would you like an ice-cream soda, or something, before you go home?

EMILY:

Well, thank you . . . I would.

They advance toward the audience and make an abrupt right turn, opening the door of Morgan's drugstore. Under strong emotion, EMILY *keeps her face down.* GEORGE *speaks to some passersby.*

GEORGE:

Hello, Stew,—how are you? —Good afternoon, Mrs. Slocum.

The STAGE MANAGER, *wearing spectacles and assuming the role of Mr. Morgan, enters abruptly from the right and stands between the audience and the counter of his soda fountain.*

STAGE MANAGER:

Hello, George. Hello, Emily. —What'll you have? —Why, Emily Webb—what you been crying about?

GEORGE:

He gropes for an explanation.

She . . . she just got an awful scare, Mr. Morgan. She almost got run over by that hardware-store wagon. Everybody says that Tom Huckins drives like a crazy man.

STAGE MANAGER:

Drawing a drink of water.

Well, now! You take a drink of water, Emily. You look all shook up. I tell you, you've got to look both ways before you cross Main Street these days. Gets worse every year. —What'll you have?

EMILY:

I'll have a strawberry phosphate, thank you, Mr. Morgan.

GEORGE:

No, no, Emily. Have an ice-cream soda with me. Two strawberry ice-cream sodas, Mr. Morgan.

STAGE MANAGER:

Working the faucets.

Two strawberry ice-cream sodas, yes, sir. Yes, sir. There are a hundred and twenty-five horses in Grover's Corners this minute I'm talking to you. State Inspector was in here yesterday. And now they're bringing in these auto-mobiles, the best thing to do is to just stay home. Why, I can remember when a dog could go to sleep all day in the middle of Main Street and nothing come along to disturb him.

He sets the imaginary glasses before them.

There they are. Enjoy 'em.

He sees a customer, right.

Yes, Mrs. Ellis. What can I do for you?

He goes out right.

EMILY:

They're so expensive.

GEORGE:

No, no,—don't you think of that. We're celebrating our election.
And then do you know what else I'm celebrating?

EMILY:

N-no.

GEORGE:

I'm celebrating because I've got a friend who tells me all the things that ought to be told me.

EMILY:

George, *please* don't think of that. I don't know why I said it. It's not true. You're—

GEORGE:

No, Emily, you stick to it. I'm glad you spoke to me like you did. But you'll *see*: I'm going to change so quick—you bet I'm going to change. And, Emily, I want to ask you a favor.

EMILY:

What?

GEORGE:

Emily, if I go away to State Agriculture College next year, will you write me a letter once in a while?

EMILY:

I certainly will. I certainly will, George. . . .

Pause. They start sipping the sodas through the straws.

It certainly seems like being away three years you'd get out of touch with things. Maybe letters from Grover's Corners wouldn't be so interesting after a while. Grover's Corners isn't a very important place when you think of all—New Hampshire; but I think it's a very nice town.

GEORGE:

The day wouldn't come when I wouldn't want to know everything that's happening here. I know *that's* true, Emily.

EMILY:

Well, I'll try to make my letters interesting.

Pause.

GEORGE:

Y'know, Emily, whenever I meet a farmer I ask him if he thinks it's important to go to Agriculture School to be a good farmer.

EMILY:

Why, George—

GEORGE:

Yeah, and some of them say that it's even a waste of time. You can get all those things, anyway, out of the pamphlets the government sends out. And Uncle Luke's getting old—he's about ready for me to start in taking over his farm tomorrow, if I could.

EMILY:

My!

GEORGE:

And, like you say, being gone all that time . . . in other

places and meeting other people . . . Gosh, if anything like that can happen I don't want to go away. I guess new people aren't any better than old ones. I'll bet they almost never are. Emily . . . I feel that you're as good a friend as I've got. I don't need to go and meet the people in other towns.

EMILY:

But, George, maybe it's very important for you to go and learn all that about—cattle judging and soils and those things. . . . Of course, I don't know.

GEORGE:

After a pause, very seriously.

Emily, I'm going to make up my mind right now. I won't go. I'll tell Pa about it tonight.

EMILY:

Why, George, I don't see why you have to decide right now. It's a whole year away.

GEORGE:

Emily, I'm glad you spoke to me about that . . . that fault in my character. What you said was right; but there was *one* thing wrong in it, and that was when you said that for a year I wasn't noticing people, and . . . you, for instance. Why, you say you were watching me when I did everything. . . . I was doing the same about you all the time.

Why, sure, —I always thought about you as one of the chief people I thought about. I always made sure where you were sitting on the bleachers, and who you were with, and for three days now I've been trying to walk home with you; but something's always got in the way. Yesterday I was standing over against the wall waiting for you, and you walked home with *Miss Corcoran*.

EMILY:

George! . . . Life's awful funny! How could I have known that? Why, I thought—

GEORGE:

Listen, Emily, I'm going to tell you why I'm not going to Agriculture School. I think that once you've found a person that you're very fond of . . . I mean a person who's fond of you, too, and likes you enough to be interested in your character . . . Well, I think that's just as important as college is, and even more so. That's what I think.

EMILY:

I think it's awfully important, too.

GEORGE:

Emily.

EMILY:

Y-yes, George.

GEORGE:

Emily, if I *do* improve and make a big change . . . would you be . . . I mean: *could* you be . . .

EMILY:

I . . . I am now; I always have been.

GEORGE:

Pause.

So I guess this is an important talk we've been having.

EMILY:

Yes . . . yes.

GEORGE:

Takes a deep breath and straightens his back.

Wait just a minute and I'll walk you home.

With mounting alarm he digs into his pockets for the money.

The STAGE MANAGER *enters, right.*

GEORGE *is deeply embarrassed, but direct.*

Mr. Morgan, I'll have to go home and get the money to pay you for this. It'll only take me a minute.

STAGE MANAGER:

Pretending to be affronted.

What's that? George Gibbs, do you mean to tell me—!

GEORGE:

Yes, but I had reasons, Mr. Morgan. —Look, here's my gold watch to keep until I come back with the money.

STAGE MANAGER:

That's all right. Keep your watch. I'll trust you.

GEORGE:

I'll be back in five minutes.

STAGE MANAGER:

I'll trust you ten years, George, —not a day over. —Got all over your shock, Emily?

EMILY:

Yes, thank you, Mr. Morgan. It was nothing.

GEORGE:

Taking up the books from the counter.

I'm ready.

They walk in grave silence across the stage and pass through the trellis at the Webbs' back door and disappear.

The STAGE MANAGER *watches them go out, then turns to the audience, removing his spectacles.*

STAGE MANAGER:

Well—

He claps his hands as a signal.

Now we're ready to get on with the wedding.

He stands waiting while the set is prepared for the next scene. Stagehands remove the chairs, tables, and trellises from the Gibbs and Webb houses.

They arrange the pews for the church in the center of the stage. The congregation will sit facing the back wall. The aisle of the church starts at the center of the back wall and comes toward the audience.

A small platform is placed against the back wall on which the STAGE MANAGER *will stand later, playing the minister. The image of a stained-glass window is cast from a lantern slide upon the back wall.*

When all is ready the STAGE MANAGER *strolls to the center of the stage, down front, and, musingly, addresses the audience.*

There are a lot of things to be said about a wedding; there are a lot of thoughts that go on during a wedding.

We can't get them all into one wedding, naturally, and especially not into a wedding at Grover's Corners, where they're awfully plain and short.

In this wedding I play the minister. That gives me the right to say a few more things about it.

For a while now, the play gets pretty serious.

Y'see, some churches say that marriage is a sacrament. I don't quite know what that means, but I can guess. Like Mrs. Gibbs said a few minutes ago: People were made to live two by two.

This is a good wedding, but people are so put together that even at a good wedding there's a lot of confusion way down deep in people's minds and we thought that that ought to be in our play, too.

The real hero of this scene isn't on the stage at all, and you know who that is. It's like what one of those European fellas said: every child born into the world is nature's attempt to make a perfect human being. Well, we've seen nature pushing and contriving for some time now. We all know

that nature's interested in quantity; but I think she's interested in quality, too—that's why I'm in the ministry.
And don't forget all the other witnesses at this wedding—the ancestors. Millions of them. Most of them set out to live two by two, also. Millions of them.
Well, that's all my sermon. 'Twan't very long, anyway.

The organ starts playing Handel's "Largo."

The congregation streams into the church and sits in silence.

Church bells are heard.

MRS. GIBBS *sits in the front row, the first seat on the aisle, the right section; next to her are* REBECCA *and* DR. GIBBS. *Across the aisle* WALLY *and* MR. WEBB. *A small choir takes its place, facing the audience under the stained-glass window.*

MRS. WEBB, *on the way to her place beside* WALLY, *turns back and speaks to the audience.*

MRS. WEBB:

I don't know why on earth I should be crying. I suppose there's nothing to cry about. It came over me at breakfast this morning; there was Emily eating her breakfast as she's done for seventeen years and now she's going off to eat it in someone else's house. I suppose that's it.
And Emily! She suddenly said: I can't eat another mouthful, and she put her head down on the table and *she* cried.

She starts toward her seat in the church, but turns back.

Oh, I've got to say it: you know, there's something downright cruel about sending our girls out into marriage this way.
I hope some of her girl friends have told her a thing or two. It's cruel, I know, but I couldn't bring myself to say anything. I went into it blind as a bat myself.

In half-amused exasperation.

The whole world's wrong, that's what's the matter.

There they come.

She hurries to her place in the pew.

GEORGE *starts to come down the right aisle of the theatre, through the audience.*

Suddenly three members of his baseball team appear by the right proscenium pillar and start whistling and catcalling to him. They are dressed for the ball field.

BASEBALL PLAYERS:

Eh, George, George! Hast—yaow! Look at him, fellas—he looks scared to death. Yaow! George, don't look so innocent, you old geezer. We know what you're thinking. Don't disgrace the team, big boy. Whoo-oo-oo.

STAGE MANAGER:

All right! All right! That'll do. That's enough of that.

Smiling, he pushes them off the stage. They lean back to shout a few more catcalls.

There used to be an awful lot of that kind of thing at weddings in the old days—Rome, and later. We're more civilized now, —so they say.

The choir starts singing "Love Divine, All Love Excelling." GEORGE *has reached the stage. He stares at the congregation a moment, then takes a few steps of withdrawal, toward the right proscenium pillar. His mother, from the front row, seems to have felt his confusion. She leaves her seat and comes down the aisle quickly to him.*

MRS. GIBBS:

George! George! What's the matter?

GEORGE:

Ma, I don't want to grow old. Why's everybody pushing me so?

MRS. GIBBS:

Why, George . . . you wanted it.

GEORGE:

No, Ma, listen to me—

MRS. GIBBS:

No, no, George, —you're a man now.

GEORGE:

Listen, Ma, —for the last time I ask you . . . All I want to do is to be a fella—

MRS. GIBBS:

George! If anyone should hear you! Now stop. Why, I'm ashamed of you!

GEORGE:

He comes to himself and looks over the scene.

What? Where's Emily?

MRS. GIBBS:

Relieved.

George! You gave me such a turn.

GEORGE:

Cheer up, Ma. I'm getting married.

MRS. GIBBS:

Let me catch my breath a minute.

GEORGE:

Comforting her.

Now, Ma, you save Thursday nights. Emily and I are coming over to dinner every Thursday night . . . you'll see. Ma, what are you crying for? Come on; we've got to get ready for this.

MRS. GIBBS, *mastering her emotion, fixes his tie and whispers to him.*

In the meantime, EMILY, *in white and wearing her wedding veil, has come through the audience and mounted onto the stage. She too draws back, frightened, when she sees the congregation in the church. The choir begins "Blessed Be the Tie That Binds."*

EMILY:

I never felt so alone in my whole life. And George over there, looking so . . . ! I *hate* him. I wish I were dead. Papa! Papa!

MR. WEBB *leaves his seat in the pews and comes toward her anxiously.*

MR. WEBB:

Emily! Emily! Now don't get upset. . . .

EMILY:

But, Papa, —I don't want to get married. . . .

MR. WEBB:

Sh—sh—Emily. Everything's all right.

EMILY:

Why can't I stay for a while just as I am? Let's go away—

MR. WEBB:

No, no, Emily. Now stop and think a minute.

EMILY:

Don't you remember that you used to say, —all the time you used to say—all the time: that I was *your* girl! There must be lots of places we can go to. I'll work for you. I could keep house.

MR. WEBB:

Sh. . . . You mustn't think of such things. You're just nervous, Emily.

He turns and calls.

George! George! Will you come here a minute?

He leads her toward George.

Why, you're marrying the best young fellow in the world. George is a fine fellow.

EMILY:

But Papa—

MRS. GIBBS *returns unobtrusively to her seat.*

MR. WEBB *has one arm around his daughter. He places his hand on George's shoulder.*

MR. WEBB:

I'm giving away my daughter, George. Do you think you can take care of her?

GEORGE:

Mr. Webb, I want to . . . I want to try. Emily, I'm going to do my best. I love you, Emily. I need you.

EMILY:

Well, if you love me, help me. All I want is someone to love me.

GEORGE:

I will, Emily. Emily, I'll try.

EMILY:

And I mean for *ever*. Do you hear? For ever and ever.

They fall into each other's arms.

The march from Lohengrin *is heard.*

The STAGE MANAGER, *as clergyman, stands on the box, up center.*

MR. WEBB:

Come, they're waiting for us. Now you know it'll be all right. Come, quick.

GEORGE *slips away and takes his place beside the* STAGE MANAGER.

EMILY *proceeds up the aisle on her father's arm.*

STAGE MANAGER:

Do you, George, take this woman, Emily, to be your wedded wife, to have . . .

MRS. SOAMES *has been sitting in the last row of the congregation.*
She now turns to her neighbors and speaks in a shrill voice. Her chatter drowns out the rest of the clergyman's words.

MRS. SOAMES:

Perfectly lovely wedding! Loveliest wedding I ever saw. Oh, I do love a good wedding, don't you? Doesn't she make a lovely bride?

GEORGE:

I do.

STAGE MANAGER:

Do you, Emily, take this man, George, to be your wedded husband . . .

Again his further words are covered by those of MRS. SOAMES.

MRS. SOAMES:

Don't know *when* I've seen such a lovely wedding. But I always cry. Don't know why it is, but I always cry. I just like to see young people happy, don't you? Oh, I think it's lovely.

The ring.

The kiss.

The stage is suddenly arrested into silent tableau.

STAGE MANAGER:

His eyes on the distance, as though to himself.

I've married over two hundred couples in my day.
Do I believe in it?
I don't know.
M. . . . marries N. . . . —millions of them.
The cottage, the go-cart, the Sunday afternoon drives in the Ford, the first rheumatism, the grandchildren, the second rheumatism, the deathbed, the reading of the will—

He now looks at the audience for the first time, with a warm smile that removes any sense of cynicism from the next line.

Once in a thousand times it's interesting.
—Well, let's have Mendelssohn's "Wedding March"!

The organ picks up the march.

The bride and groom come down the aisle, radiant, but trying to be very dignified.

MRS. SOAMES:

Aren't they a lovely couple? Oh, I've never been to such a nice wedding. I'm sure they'll be happy. I always say: *happiness*, that's the great thing! The important thing is to be happy.

The bride and groom reach the steps leading into the audience.

A bright light is thrown upon them. They descend into the auditorium and run up the aisle joyously.

STAGE MANAGER:

That's all the Second Act, folks. Ten minutes' intermission.

Act Three

·⁘·⁘·⁘·⁘·⁘·

During the intermission the audience has seen the stagehands arranging the stage. On the right-hand side, a little right of the center, ten or twelve ordinary chairs have been placed in three openly spaced rows facing the audience.
These are graves in the cemetery.
Toward the end of the intermission the actors enter and take their places. The front row contains: toward the center of the stage, an empty chair; then MRS. GIBBS; SIMON STIMSON.
The second row contains among others, MRS. SOAMES.
The third row has WALLY WEBB.
The dead do not turn their heads or their eyes to right or left, but they sit in a quiet without stiffness. When they speak, their tone is matter-of-fact, without sentimentality and, above all, without lugubriousness.
The STAGE MANAGER *takes his accustomed place and waits for the houselights to go down.*

STAGE MANAGER:

This time nine years have gone by, friends—summer, 1913. Gradual changes in Grover's Corners. Horses are getting rarer. Farmers coming into town in Fords.
Everybody locks their house doors now at night. Ain't been any burglars in town yet, but everybody's heard about 'em.
You'd be surprised, though—on the whole, things don't change much around here.

This is certainly an important part of Grover's Corners. It's on a hilltop—a windy hilltop—lots of sky, lots of clouds, —often lots of sun and moon and stars.
You come up here on a fine afternoon and you can see range on range of hills—awful blue they are—up there by Lake Sunapee and Lake Winnipesaukee . . . and way up, if you've got a glass, you can see the White Mountains and Mt. Washington—where North Conway and Conway is. And, of course, our favorite mountain, Mt. Monadnock, 's right here—and all these towns that lie around it: Jaffrey, 'n East Jaffrey, 'n Peterborough, 'n Dublin; and

Then pointing down in the audience.

there, quite a ways down, is Grover's Corners.
Yes, beautiful spot up here. Mountain laurel and li-lacks. I often wonder why people like to be buried in Woodlawn and Brooklyn when they might pass the same time up here in New Hampshire. Over there—

Pointing to stage left.

are the old stones—1670, 1680. Strong-minded people that come a long way to be independent. Summer people walk around there laughing at the funny words on the tombstones. . . . It don't do any harm. And genealogists come up from Boston—get paid by city people for looking up their ancestors. They want to make sure they're Daughters of the American Revolution and of the *Mayflower*. . . . Well, I guess that don't do any harm, either. Wherever you come near the human race, there's layers and layers of nonsense. . . .
Over there are some Civil War veterans. Iron flags on their graves . . . New Hampshire boys . . . had a notion that the Union ought to be kept together, though they'd never

seen more than fifty miles of it themselves. All they knew was the name, friends—the United States of America. The United States of America. And they went and died about it.

This here is the new part of the cemetery. Here's your friend Mrs. Gibbs. 'N let me see— Here's Mr. Stimson, organist at the Congregational Church. And Mrs. Soames who enjoyed the wedding so—you remember? Oh, and a lot of others. And Editor Webb's boy, Wallace, whose appendix burst while he was on a Boy Scout trip to Crawford Notch.

Yes, an awful lot of sorrow has sort of quieted down up here. People just wild with grief have brought their relatives up to this hill. We all know how it is . . . and then time . . . and sunny days . . . and rainy days . . . 'n snow . . . We're all glad they're in a beautiful place and we're coming up here ourselves when our fit's over.

Now there are some things we all know, but we don't take'm out and look at'm very often. We all know that *something* is eternal. And it ain't houses and it ain't names, and it ain't earth, and it ain't even the stars. . . . Everybody knows in their bones that *something* is eternal, and that something has to do with human beings. All the greatest people ever lived have been telling us that for five thousand years and yet you'd be surprised how people are always losing hold of it. There's something way down deep that's eternal about every human being.

Pause.

You know as well as I do that the dead don't stay interested in us living people for very long. Gradually, gradually, they lose hold of the earth . . . and the ambitions

they had . . . and the pleasures they had . . . and the things they suffered . . . and the people they loved.
They get weaned away from earth—that's the way I put it, —weaned away.
And they stay here while the earth part of 'em burns away, burns out; and all that time they slowly get indifferent to what's goin' on in Grover's Corners.
They're waitin'. They're waitin' for something that they feel is comin'. Something important, and great. Aren't they waitin' for the eternal part in them to come out clear?
Some of the things they're going to say maybe'll hurt your feelings—but that's the way it is: mother 'n daughter . . . husband 'n wife . . . enemy 'n enemy . . . money 'n miser . . . all those terribly important things kind of grow pale around here. And what's left when memory's gone, and your identity, Mrs. Smith?

He looks at the audience a minute, then turns to the stage.

Well! There are some *living* people. There's Joe Stoddard, our undertaker, supervising a new-made grave. And here comes a Grover's Corners boy, that left town to go out West.

JOE STODDARD *has hovered about in the background.* SAM CRAIG *enters left, wiping his forehead from the exertion. He carries an umbrella and strolls front.*

SAM CRAIG:

Good afternoon, Joe Stoddard.

JOE STODDARD:

Good afternoon, good afternoon. Let me see now: do I know you?

SAM CRAIG:

I'm Sam Craig.

JOE STODDARD:

Gracious sakes' alive! Of all people! I should'a knowed you'd be back for the funeral. You've been away a long time, Sam.

SAM CRAIG:

Yes, I've been away over twelve years. I'm in business out in Buffalo now, Joe. But I was in the East when I got news of my cousin's death, so I thought I'd combine things a little and come and see the old home. You look well.

JOE STODDARD:

Yes, yes, can't complain. Very sad, our journey today, Samuel.

SAM CRAIG:

Yes.

JOE STODDARD:

Yes, yes. I always say I hate to supervise when a young person is taken. They'll be here in a few minutes now. I had to come here early today—my son's supervisin' at the home.

SAM CRAIG:

Reading stones.

Old Farmer McCarty, I used to do chores for him—after school. He had the lumbago.

JOE STODDARD:

Yes, we brought Farmer McCarty here a number of years ago now.

SAM CRAIG:

Staring at Mrs. Gibbs' knees.
Why, this is my Aunt Julia. . . . I'd forgotten that she'd . . . of course, of course.

JOE STODDARD:

Yes, Doc Gibbs lost his wife two-three years ago . . . about this time. And today's another pretty bad blow for him, too.

MRS. GIBBS:

To SIMON STIMSON: *in an even voice.*
That's my sister Carey's boy, Sam . . . Sam Craig.

SIMON STIMSON:

I'm always uncomfortable when *they're* around.

MRS. GIBBS:

Simon.

SAM CRAIG:

Do they choose their own verses much, Joe?

JOE STODDARD:

No . . . not usual. Mostly the bereaved pick a verse.

SAM CRAIG:

Doesn't sound like Aunt Julia. There aren't many of those Hersey sisters left now. Let me see: where are . . . I wanted to look at my father's and mother's . . .

JOE STODDARD:

Over there with the Craigs . . . Avenue F.

SAM CRAIG:

Reading Simon Stimson's epitaph.
He was organist at church, wasn't he? —Hm, drank a lot, we used to say.

JOE STODDARD:

Nobody was supposed to know about it. He'd seen a peck of trouble.
Behind his hand.
Took his own life, y' know?

SAM CRAIG:

Oh, did he?

JOE STODDARD:

Hung himself in the attic. They tried to hush it up, but of course it got around. He chose his own epy-taph. You can see it there. It ain't a verse exactly.

SAM CRAIG:

Why, it's just some notes of music—what is it?

JOE STODDARD:

Oh, I wouldn't know. It was wrote up in the Boston papers at the time.

SAM CRAIG:

Joe, what did she die of?

JOE STODDARD:

Who?

SAM CRAIG:

My cousin.

JOE STODDARD:

Oh, didn't you know? Had some trouble bringing a baby into the world. 'Twas her second, though. There's a little boy 'bout four years old.

SAM CRAIG:

Opening his umbrella.

The grave's going to be over there?

JOE STODDARD:

Yes, there ain't much more room over here among the Gibbses, so they're opening up a whole new Gibbs section over by Avenue B.

You'll excuse me now. I see they're comin'.

From left to center, at the back of the stage, comes a procession. Four men carry a casket, invisible to us. All the rest are under umbrellas. One can vaguely see: DR. GIBBS, GEORGE, *the* WEBBS, *etc. They gather about a grave in the back center of the stage, a little to the left of center.*

MRS. SOAMES:

Who is it, Julia?

MRS. GIBBS:

Without raising her eyes.

My daughter-in-law, Emily Webb.

MRS. SOAMES:

A little surprised, but no emotion.

Well, I declare! The road up here must have been awful muddy.

What did she die of, Julia?

MRS. GIBBS:

In childbirth.

MRS. SOAMES:

Childbirth.

Almost with a laugh.

I'd forgotten all about that. My, wasn't life awful—

With a sigh.

and wonderful.

SIMON STIMSON:

With a sideways glance.

Wonderful, was it?

MRS. GIBBS:

Simon! Now, remember!

MRS. SOAMES:

I remember Emily's wedding. Wasn't it a lovely wedding! And I remember her reading the class poem at Graduation Exercises. Emily was one of the brightest girls ever graduated from High School. I've heard Principal Wilkins say so time after time. I called on them at their new farm, just before I died. Perfectly beautiful farm.

A WOMAN AMONG THE DEAD:

It's on the same road we lived on.

A MAN AMONG THE DEAD:

Yepp, right smart farm.

They subside. The group by the grave starts singing "Blessed Be the Tie That Binds."

A WOMAN AMONG THE DEAD:

I always liked that hymn. I was hopin' they'd sing a hymn.

Pause. Suddenly EMILY *appears from among the umbrellas. She is wearing a white dress. Her hair is down her back and tied by a white ribbon like a little girl. She comes slowly, gazing wondering at the dead, a little dazed. She stops halfway and smiles faintly. After looking at the mourners for a moment, she walks slowly to the vacant chair beside* MRS. GIBBS *and sits down.*

EMILY:

To them all, quietly, smiling.

Hello.

MRS. SOAMES:

Hello, Emily.

A MAN AMONG THE DEAD:

Hello, M's Gibbs.

EMILY:

Warmly.

Hello, Mother Gibbs.

MRS. GIBBS:

Emily.

EMILY:

Hello.

With surprise.

It's raining.

Her eyes drift back to the funeral company.

MRS. GIBBS:

Yes. . . . They'll be gone soon, dear. Just rest yourself.

EMILY:

It seems thousands and thousands of years since I . . .
Papa remembered that that was my favorite hymn.
Oh, I wish I'd been here a long time. I don't like being new here. —How do you do, Mr. Stimson?

SIMON STIMSON:

How do you do, Emily.

EMILY *continues to look about her with a wondering smile; as though to shut out from her mind the thought of the funeral company, she starts speaking to* MRS. GIBBS *with a touch of nervousness.*

EMILY:

Mother Gibbs, George and I have made that farm into just the best place you ever saw. We thought of you all the time. We wanted to show you the new barn and a great long ce-ment drinking fountain for the stock. We bought that out of the money you left us.

MRS. GIBBS:

I did?

EMILY:

Don't you remember, Mother Gibbs—the legacy you left us? Why, it was over three hundred and fifty dollars.

MRS. GIBBS:

Yes, yes, Emily.

EMILY:

Well, there's a patent device on the drinking fountain so that it never overflows, Mother Gibbs, and it never sinks below a certain mark they have there. It's fine.

Her voice trails off and her eyes return to the funeral group.

It won't be the same to George without me, but it's a lovely farm.

Suddenly she looks directly at MRS. GIBBS.

Live people don't understand, do they?

MRS. GIBBS:

No, dear—not very much.

EMILY:

They're sort of shut up in little boxes, aren't they? I feel as though I knew them last a thousand years ago. . . . My boy is spending the day at Mrs. Carter's.

She sees MR. CARTER *among the dead.*

Oh, Mr. Carter, my little boy is spending the day at your house.

MR. CARTER:

Is he?

EMILY:

Yes, he loves it there. —Mother Gibbs, we have a Ford, too. Never gives any trouble. I don't drive, though. Mother Gibbs, when does this feeling go away? —Of being . . . one of *them?* How long does it . . . ?

MRS. GIBBS:

Sh! dear. Just wait and be patient.

EMILY:

With a sigh.

I know. —Look, they're finished. They're going.

MRS. GIBBS:

Sh—.

The umbrellas leave the stage. DR. GIBBS *has come over to his wife's grave and stands before it a moment.* EMILY *looks up at his face.* MRS. GIBBS *does not raise her eyes.*

EMILY:

Look! Father Gibbs is bringing some of my flowers to you. He looks just like George, doesn't he? Oh, Mother Gibbs, I never realized before how troubled and how . . . how in the dark live persons are. Look at him. I loved him so. From morning till night, that's all they are—troubled.

DR. GIBBS *goes off.*

THE DEAD:

Little cooler than it was. —Yes, that rain's cooled it off a little. Those northeast winds always do the same thing, don't they? If it isn't rain, it's a three-day blow.

A patient calm falls on the stage. The STAGE MANAGER *appears at his proscenium pillar, smoking.* EMILY *sits up abruptly with an idea.*

EMILY:

But, Mother Gibbs, one can go back; one can go back there again . . . into living. I feel it. I know it. Why, just then for a moment I was thinking about . . . about the farm . . . and for a minute I *was* there, and my baby was on my lap as plain as day.

MRS. GIBBS:

Yes, of course you can.

EMILY:

I can go back there and live all those days over again . . . why not?

MRS. GIBBS:

All I can say is, Emily, don't.

EMILY:

She appeals urgently to the STAGE MANAGER.

But it's true, isn't it? I can go and live . . . back there . . . again.

STAGE MANAGER:

Yes, some have tried—but they soon come back here.

MRS. GIBBS:

Don't do it, Emily.

MRS. SOAMES:

Emily, don't. It's not what you think it'd be.

EMILY:

But I won't live over a sad day. I'll choose a happy one—I'll choose the day I first knew that I loved George. Why should that be painful?

They are silent. Her question turns to the STAGE MANAGER.

STAGE MANAGER:

You not only live it; but you watch yourself living it.

EMILY:

Yes?

STAGE MANAGER:

And as you watch it, you see the thing that they—down there—never know. You see the future. You know what's going to happen afterwards.

EMILY:

But is that—painful? Why?

MRS. GIBBS:

That's not the only reason why you shouldn't do it, Emily. When you've been here longer you'll see that our life here is to forget all that, and think only of what's ahead, and be ready for what's ahead. When you've been here longer you'll understand.

EMILY:

Softly.

But, Mother Gibbs, how can I *ever* forget that life? It's all I know. It's all I had.

MRS. SOAMES:

Oh, Emily. It isn't wise. Really, it isn't.

EMILY:

But it's a thing I must know for myself. I'll choose a happy day, anyway.

MRS. GIBBS:

No! —At least, choose an unimportant day. Choose the least important day in your life. It will be important enough.

EMILY:

To herself.

Then it can't be since I was married; or since the baby was born.

To the STAGE MANAGER, *eagerly.*

I can choose a birthday at least, can't I? —I choose my twelfth birthday.

STAGE MANAGER:

All right. February 11th, 1899. A Tuesday. —Do you want any special time of day?

EMILY:

Oh, I want the whole day.

STAGE MANAGER:

We'll begin at dawn. You remember it had been snowing for several days; but it had stopped the night before, and they had begun clearing the roads. The sun's coming up.

EMILY:

With a cry; rising.

There's Main Street. . . . Why, that's Mr. Morgan's drugstore before he changed it! . . . And there's the livery stable.

The stage at no time in this act has been very dark; but now the left half of the stage gradually becomes very bright—the brightness of a crisp winter morning.
EMILY *walks toward Main Street.*

STAGE MANAGER:

Yes, it's 1899. This is fourteen years ago.

EMILY:

Oh, that's the town I knew as a little girl. And, *look*, there's the old white fence that used to be around our house. Oh, I'd forgotten that! Oh, I love it so! Are they inside?

STAGE MANAGER:

Yes, your mother'll be coming downstairs in a minute to make breakfast.

EMILY:

Softly.
Will she?

STAGE MANAGER:

And you remember: your father had been away for several days; he came back on the early-morning train.

EMILY:

No . . . ?

STAGE MANAGER:

He'd been back to his college to make a speech—in western New York, at Clinton.

EMILY:

Look! There's Howie Newsome. There's our policeman. But he's *dead*; he *died*.

The voices of HOWIE NEWSOME, CONSTABLE WARREN, *and* JOE CROWELL, JR., *are heard at the left of the stage.* EMILY *listens in delight.*

HOWIE NEWSOME:

Whoa, Bessie! —Bessie! 'Morning, Bill.

CONSTABLE WARREN:

Morning, Howie.

HOWIE NEWSOME:

You're up early.

CONSTABLE WARREN:

Been rescuin' a party; darn near froze to death, down by Polish Town thar. Got drunk and lay out in the snow-drifts. Thought he was in bed when I shook'm.

EMILY:

Why, there's Joe Crowell. . . .

JOE CROWELL, JR.:

Good morning, Mr. Warren. 'Morning, Howie.

MRS. WEBB *has appeared in her kitchen, but* EMILY *does not see her until she calls.*

MRS. WEBB:

Chil-*dren!* Wally! Emily! . . . Time to get up.

EMILY:

Mama, I'm here! Oh! how young Mama looks! I didn't know Mama was ever that young.

MRS. WEBB:

You can come and dress by the kitchen fire, if you like; but hurry.

HOWIE NEWSOME *has entered along Main Street and brings the milk to Mrs. Webb's door.*

Good morning, Mr. Newsome. Whhhh—it's cold.

HOWIE NEWSOME:

Ten below by my barn, Mrs. Webb.

MRS. WEBB:

Think of it! Keep yourself wrapped up.

She takes her bottles in, shuddering.

EMILY:

With an effort.

Mama, I can't find my blue hair ribbon anywhere.

MRS. WEBB:

Just open your eyes, dear, that's all. I laid it out for you special—on the dresser, there. If it were a snake it would bite you.

EMILY:

Yes, yes . . .

She puts her hand on her heart. MR. WEBB *comes along Main*

Street, where he meets CONSTABLE WARREN. *Their movements and voices are increasingly lively in the sharp air.*

MR. WEBB:

Good morning, Bill.

CONSTABLE WARREN:

Good morning, Mr. Webb. You're up early.

MR. WEBB:

Yes, just been back to my old college in New York State. Been any trouble here?

CONSTABLE WARREN:

Well, I was called up this mornin' to rescue a Polish fella—darn near froze to death he was.

MR. WEBB:

We must get it in the paper.

CONSTABLE WARREN:

'Twan't much.

EMILY:

Whispers.

Papa.

MR. WEBB *shakes the snow off his feet and enters his house.* CONSTABLE WARREN *goes off, right.*

MR. WEBB:

Good morning, Mother.

MRS. WEBB:

How did it go, Charles?

MR. WEBB:

Oh, fine, I guess. I told'm a few things. —Everything all right here?

MRS. WEBB:

Yes—can't think of anything that's happened, special. Been right cold. Howie Newsome says it's ten below over to his barn.

MR. WEBB:

Yes, well, it's colder than that at Hamilton College. Students' ears are falling off. It ain't Christian. —Paper have any mistakes in it?

MRS. WEBB:

None that I noticed. Coffee's ready when you want it.

He starts upstairs.

Charles! Don't forget; it's Emily's birthday. Did you remember to get her something?

MR. WEBB:

Patting his pocket.

Yes, I've got something here.

Calling up the stairs.

Where's my girl? Where's my birthday girl?

He goes off left.

MRS. WEBB:

Don't interrupt her now, Charles. You can see her at breakfast. She's slow enough as it is. Hurry up, children! It's seven o'clock. Now, I don't want to call you again.

EMILY:

Softly, more in wonder than in grief.

I can't bear it. They're so young and beautiful. Why did they ever have to get old? Mama, I'm here. I'm grown up. I love you all, everything. —I can't look at everything hard enough.

She looks questioningly at the STAGE MANAGER, *saying or suggesting: "Can I go in?" He nods briefly. She crosses to the inner door to the kitchen, left of her mother, as though entering the room. Suggesting the voice of a girl of twelve.*

Good morning, Mama.

MRS. WEBB:

Crossing to embrace and kiss her; in her characteristic matter-of-fact manner.

Well, now, dear, a very happy birthday to my girl and many happy returns. There are some surprises waiting for you on the kitchen table.

EMILY:

Oh, Mama, you *shouldn't* have.

She throws an anguished glance at the STAGE MANAGER.

I can't—I can't.

MRS. WEBB:

Facing the audience, over her stove.

But birthday or no birthday, I want you to eat your breakfast good and slow. I want you to grow up and be a good strong girl.
That in the blue paper is from your Aunt Carrie; and I reckon you can guess who brought the postcard album. I found it on the doorstep when I brought in the milk—George Gibbs . . . must have come over in the cold pretty early . . . right nice of him.

EMILY:

To herself.
Oh, George! I'd forgotten that. . . .

MRS. WEBB:

Chew that bacon good and slow. It'll help keep you warm on a cold day.

EMILY:

With mounting urgency.
Oh, Mama, just look at me one minute as though you really saw me. Mama, fourteen years have gone by. I'm dead. You're a grandmother, Mama. I married George Gibbs, Mama. Wally's dead, too. Mama, his appendix burst on a camping trip to North Conway. We felt just terrible about it—don't you remember? But, just for a moment now we're all together. Mama, just for a moment we're happy. *Let's look at one another*.

MRS. WEBB:

That in the yellow paper is something I found in the attic

among your grandmother's things. You're old enough to wear it now, and I thought you'd like it.

EMILY:

And this is from you. Why, Mama, it's just lovely and it's just what I wanted. It's beautiful!

She flings her arms around her mother's neck. Her mother goes on with her cooking, but is pleased.

MRS. WEBB:

Well, I hoped you'd like it. Hunted all over. Your Aunt Norah couldn't find one in Concord, so I had to send all the way to Boston.

Laughing.

Wally has something for you, too. He made it at manual-training class and he's very proud of it. Be sure you make a big fuss about it. —Your father has a surprise for you, too; don't know what it is myself. Sh—here he comes.

MR. WEBB:

Offstage.

Where's my girl? Where's my birthday girl?

EMILY:

In a loud voice to the STAGE MANAGER.

I can't. I can't go on. It goes so fast. We don't have time to look at one another.

She breaks down sobbing.

The lights dim on the left half of the stage. MRS. WEBB *disappears.*

I didn't realize. So all that was going on and we never noticed. Take me back—up the hill—to my grave. But first: Wait! One more look.

Good-by, good-by, world. Good-by, Grover's Corners . . . Mama and Papa. Good-by to clocks ticking . . . and Mama's sunflowers. And food and coffee. And new-ironed dresses and hot baths . . . and sleeping and waking up. Oh, earth, you're too wonderful for anybody to realize you.

She looks toward the STAGE MANAGER; *abruptly, through her tears.*

Do any human beings ever realize life while they live it?—every, every minute?

STAGE MANAGER:

No.

Pause.

The saints and poets, maybe—they do some.

EMILY:

I'm ready to go back.

She returns to her chair beside MRS. GIBBS.

Pause.

MRS. GIBBS:

Were you happy?

EMILY:

No . . . I should have listened to you. That's all human beings are! Just blind people.

MRS. GIBBS:

Look, it's clearing up. The stars are coming out.

EMILY:

Oh, Mr. Stimson, I should have listened to them.

SIMON STIMSON:

With mounting violence; bitingly.

Yes, now you know. Now you know! That's what it was to be alive. To move about in a cloud of ignorance; to go up and down trampling on the feelings of those . . . of those about you. To spend and waste time as though you had a million years. To be always at the mercy of one self-centered passion, or another. Now you know—that's the happy existence you wanted to go back to. Ignorance and blindness.

MRS. GIBBS:

Spiritedly.

Simon Stimson, that ain't the whole truth and you know it. Emily, look at that star. I forget its name.

A MAN AMONG THE DEAD:

My boy Joel was a sailor—knew 'em all. He'd set on the porch evenings and tell 'em all by name. Yes, sir, wonderful!

ANOTHER MAN AMONG THE DEAD:

A star's mighty good company.

A WOMAN AMONG THE DEAD:

Yes. Yes, 'tis.

SIMON STIMSON:

Here's one of *them* coming.

THE DEAD:

That's funny. 'Tain't no time for one of them to be here. —Goodness sakes.

EMILY:

Mother Gibbs, it's George.

MRS. GIBBS:

Sh, dear. Just rest yourself.

EMILY:

It's George.

GEORGE *enters from the left, and slowly comes toward them.*

A MAN AMONG THE DEAD:

And my boy, Joel, who knew the stars—he used to say it took millions of years for that speck o' light to git to the earth. Don't seem like a body could believe it, but that's what he used to say—millions of years.

GEORGE *sinks to his knees then falls full length at Emily's feet.*

A WOMAN AMONG THE DEAD:

Goodness! That ain't no way to behave!

MRS. SOAMES:

He ought to be home.

EMILY:

Mother Gibbs?

MRS. GIBBS:

Yes, Emily?

EMILY:

They don't understand, do they?

MRS. GIBBS:

No, dear. They don't understand.

The STAGE MANAGER *appears at the right, one hand on a dark curtain which he slowly draws across the scene.*

In the distance a clock is heard striking the hour very faintly.

STAGE MANAGER:

Most everybody's asleep in Grover's Corners. There are a few lights on: Shorty Hawkins, down at the depot, has just watched the Albany train go by. And at the livery stable somebody's setting up late and talking. —Yes, it's clearing up. There are the stars—doing their old, old crisscross journeys in the sky. Scholars haven't settled the matter yet, but they seem to think there are no living beings up there. Just chalk . . . or fire. Only this one is straining away, straining away all the time to make something of itself. The strain's so bad that every sixteen hours everybody lies down and gets a rest.

He winds his watch.

Hm. . . . Eleven o'clock in Grover's Corners. —You get a good rest, too. Good night.

THE END

The Skin of Our Teeth

A Play in Three Acts

The first performance of *The Skin of Our Teeth* took place at the Shubert Theatre in New Haven, Connecticut, on October 15, 1942. It opened in New York at the Plymouth Theatre on November 18. It was produced by Michael Myerberg and directed by Elia Kazan. Sabina was played by Tallulah Bankhead, Mr. and Mrs. Antrobus by Fredric March and Florence Eldridge, the Antrobus children by Montgomery Clift and Frances Heflin, the Fortune Teller by Florence Reed. The scenery was designed by Albert Johnson, the costumes by Mary Percy Schenck.

The London production opened at the Phoenix Theatre on May 16, 1945. It was presented by H. M. Tennent Ltd. and directed by Sir Laurence Olivier. Sabina was played by Vivien Leigh, Mr. and Mrs. Antrobus by Cecil Parker (later by George Devine) and Joan Young (later by Esther Somers), the Antrobus children by Terry Morgan and Pamela Conroy, the Fortune Teller by Ena Burrill. The scenery and costumes were designed by Roger Furse. On a tour of Australia and New Zealand in 1948, the role of Mr. Antrobus was played by Sir Laurence Olivier.

In a revival produced by the American National Theatre and Academy for presentation in Paris in June, 1955, as a part of the Festival "Salut à la France," and later presented in a number of cities in the United States, Sabina was played by Mary Martin, Mr. and Mrs. Antrobus by George Abbott and Helen Hayes, and the Fortune Teller by Florence Reed. The play was directed by Alan Schneider.

Characters

In the order of their appearance

Announcer
Sabina
Mr. Fitzpatrick
Mrs. Antrobus
Dinosaur
Telegraph Boy
Mammoth
Gladys
Henry
Mr. Antrobus
Doctor
Professor
Judge
Homer
Miss E. Muse
Miss T. Muse
Miss M. Muse
Two Ushers
Fortune Teller
Two Chair Pushers
Six Conveeners
Bingo Caller
Chorus
Broadcast Official
Mr. Tremayne
Hester
Ivy
Fred Bailey

Act I Home, Excelsior, New Jersey.
Act II Atlantic City Boardwalk.
Act III Home, Excelsior, New Jersey.

Alan E Cober

Act One

A projection screen in the middle of the curtain. The first lantern slide: the name of the theatre, and the words: NEWS EVENTS OF THE WORLD. An announcer's voice is heard.

ANNOUNCER:

The management takes pleasure in bringing to you—The News Events of the World.

Slide of the sun appearing above the horizon.

Freeport, Long Island:

The sun rose this morning at 6:32 A.M. This gratifying event was first reported by Mrs. Dorothy Stetson of Freeport, Long Island, who promptly telephoned the Mayor. The Society for Affirming the End of the World at once went into a special session and postponed the arrival of that event for TWENTY-FOUR HOURS.

All honor to Mrs. Stetson for her public spirit.

New York City:

Slide of the front doors of the theatre in which this play is playing; three cleaning women with mops and pails.

The X Theatre. During the daily cleaning of this theatre a number of lost objects were collected as usual by Mesdames Simpson, Pateslewski, and Moriarty.

Among these objects found today was a wedding ring, inscribed: To Eva from Adam. Genesis II:18.

The ring will be restored to the owner or owners, if their credentials are satisfactory.

Tippehatchee, Vermont:

Slide representing a glacier.

The unprecedented cold weather of this summer has produced a condition that has not yet been satisfactorily explained. There is a report that a wall of ice is moving southward across these counties. The disruption of communications by the cold wave now crossing the country has rendered exact information difficult, but little credence is given to the rumor that the ice had pushed the Cathedral of Montreal as far as St. Albans, Vermont.
For further information see your daily papers.

Excelsior, New Jersey:

Slide of a modest suburban home.

The home of Mr. George Antrobus, the inventor of the wheel. The discovery of the wheel, following so closely on the discovery of the lever, has centered the attention of the country on Mr. Antrobus of this attractive suburban residence district. This is his home, a commodious seven-room house, conveniently situated near a public school, a Methodist church, and a firehouse; it is right handy to an A&P.

Slide of MR. ANTROBUS *on his front steps, smiling and lifting his straw hat. He holds a wheel.*

Mr. Antrobus, himself. He comes of very old stock and has made his way up from next to nothing.
It is reported that he was once a gardener, but left that sit-

uation under circumstances that have been variously reported.
Mr. Antrobus is a veteran of foreign wars, and bears a number of scars, front and back.

Slide of MRS. ANTROBUS, *holding some roses.*

This is Mrs. Antrobus, the charming and gracious president of the Excelsior Mothers' Club.
Mrs. Antrobus is an excellent needlewoman; it is she who invented the apron on which so many interesting changes have been rung since.

Slide of the family and SABINA.

Here we see the Antrobuses with their two children, Henry and Gladys, and friend. The friend in the rear is Lily Sabina, the maid.
I know we all want to congratulate this typical American family on its enterprise. We all wish Mr. Antrobus a successful future. Now the management takes you to the interior of this home for a brief visit.

Curtain rises. Living room of a commuter's home. SABINA *— straw blonde, over-rouged—is standing by the window back center, a feather duster under her elbow.*

SABINA:

Oh, oh, oh! Six o'clock and the master not home yet.
Pray God nothing serious has happened to him crossing the Hudson River. If anything happened to him, we would certainly be inconsolable and have to move into a less desirable residence district.
The fact is I don't know what'll become of us. Here it is the middle of August and the coldest day of the year. It's

simply freezing; the dogs are sticking to the sidewalks; can anybody explain that? No.
But I'm not surprised. The whole world's at sixes and sevens, and why the house hasn't fallen down about our ears long ago is a miracle to me.

A fragment of the right wall leans precariously over the stage. SABINA *looks at it nervously and it slowly rights itself.*

Every night this same anxiety as to whether the master will get home safely: whether he'll bring home anything to eat. In the midst of life we are in the midst of death, a truer word was never said.

The fragment of scenery flies up into the lofts. SABINA *is struck dumb with surprise, shrugs her shoulders and starts dusting Mr. Antrobus' chair, including the underside.*

Of course, Mr. Antrobus is a very fine man, an excellent husband and father, a pillar of the church, and has all the best interests of the community at heart. Of course, every muscle goes tight every time he passes a policeman; but what I think is that there are certain charges that ought not to be made, and I think I may add, ought not to be allowed to be made; we're all human; who isn't?

She dusts Mrs. Antrobus' rocking chair.

Mrs. Antrobus is as fine a woman as you could hope to see. She lives only for her children; and if it would be any benefit to her children she'd see the rest of us stretched out dead at her feet without turning a hair—that's the truth. If you want to know anything more about Mrs. Antrobus, just go and look at a tigress, and look hard.
As to the children—
Well, Henry Antrobus is a real, clean-cut American boy. He'll graduate from high school one of these days, if they

make the alphabet any easier. —Henry, when he has a stone in his hand, has a perfect aim; he can hit anything from a bird to an older brother— Oh! I didn't mean to say that! —but it certainly was an unfortunate accident, and it was very hard getting the police out of the house.
Mr. and Mrs. Antrobus' daughter is named Gladys. She'll make some good man a good wife some day, if he'll just come down off the movie screen and ask her.
So here we are!
We've managed to survive for some time now, catch as catch can, the fat and the lean, and if the dinosaurs don't trample us to death, and if the grasshoppers don't eat up our garden, we'll all live to see better days, knock on wood.
Each new child that's born to the Antrobuses seems to them to be sufficient reason for the whole universe's being set in motion; and each new child that dies seems to them to have been spared a whole world of sorrow, and what the end of it will be is still very much an open question.
We've rattled along, hot and cold, for some time now—

A portion of the wall above the door, right, flies up into the air and disappears.

—and my advice to you is not to inquire into why or whither, but just enjoy your ice cream while it's on your plate, —that's my philosophy.
Don't forget that a few years ago we came through the depression by the skin of our teeth! One more tight squeeze like that and where will we be?

This is a cue line. SABINA *looks angrily at the kitchen door and repeats cue.*

. . . we came through the depression by the skin of our

teeth; one more tight squeeze like that and where will we be?

Flustered, she looks through the opening in the right wall; then goes to the window and reopens the act.

Oh, oh, oh! Six o'clock and the master not home yet. Pray God nothing has happened to him crossing the Hudson. Here it is the middle of August and the coldest day of the year. It's simply freezing; the dogs are sticking. One more tight squeeze like that and where will we be?

VOICE:

Offstage.

Make up something! Invent something!

SABINA:

Well . . . uh . . . this certainly is a fine American home . . . and—uh . . . everybody's very happy . . . and—uh . . .

Suddenly flings pretense to the winds and, coming downstage, speaks with indignation.

I can't invent any words for this play, and I'm glad I can't. I hate this play and every word in it.

As for me, I don't understand a single word of it, anyway—all about the troubles the human race has gone through, there's a subject for you.

Besides, the author hasn't made up his silly mind as to whether we're all living back in caves or in New Jersey today, and that's the way it is all the way through.

Oh—why can't we have plays like we used to have—*Peg o' My Heart*, and *Smilin' Thru*, and *The Bat*—good entertainment with a message you can take home with you?

I took this hateful job because I had to. For two years I've sat up in my room living on a sandwich and a cup of tea a day, waiting for better times in the theatre. And look at me now: I— I who've played *Rain* and *The Barretts of Wimpole Street* and *First Lady*—God in Heaven!

The STAGE MANAGER *puts his head out from the hole in the scenery.*

MR. FITZPATRICK:

Miss Somerset!! Miss Somerset!

SABINA:

Oh! Anyway! —nothing matters! It'll all be the same in a hundred years.

Loudly.

We came through the depression by the skin of our teeth, —that's true! —One more tight squeeze like that and where will we be?

Enter MRS. ANTROBUS, *a mother.*

MRS. ANTROBUS:

Sabina, you've let the fire go out.

SABINA:

In a lather.

One-thing-and-another; don't-know-whether-my-wits-are-upside-or-down; might-as-well-be-dead-as-alive-in-a-house-all-sixes-and-sevens. . . .

MRS. ANTROBUS:

You've let the fire go out. Here it is the coldest day of the year right in the middle of August, and you've let the fire go out.

SABINA:

Mrs. Antrobus, I'd like to give my two weeks' notice, Mrs. Antrobus. A girl like I can get a situation in a home where they're rich enough to have a fire in every room, Mrs. Antrobus, and a girl don't have to carry the responsibility of the whole house on her two shoulders. And a home without children, Mrs. Antrobus, because children are a thing only a parent can stand, and a truer word was never said; and a home, Mrs. Antrobus, where the master of the house don't pinch decent, self-respecting girls when he meets them in a dark corridor. I mention no names and make no charges. So you have my notice, Mrs. Antrobus. I hope that's perfectly clear.

MRS. ANTROBUS:

You've let the fire go out! —Have you milked the mammoth?

SABINA:

I don't understand a word of this play. —Yes, I've milked the mammoth.

MRS. ANTROBUS:

Until Mr. Antrobus comes home we have no food and we have no fire. You'd better go over to the neighbors and borrow some fire.

SABINA:

Mrs. Antrobus! I can't! I'd die on the way, you know I would. It's worse than January. The dogs are sticking to the sidewalks. I'd die.

MRS. ANTROBUS:

Very well, I'll go.

SABINA:

Even more distraught, coming forward and sinking on her knees.

You'd never come back alive; we'd all perish; if you weren't here, we'd just perish. How do we know Mr. Antrobus'll be back? We don't know. If you go out, I'll just kill myself.

MRS. ANTROBUS:

Get up, Sabina.

SABINA:

Every night it's the same thing. Will he come back safe, or won't he? Will we starve to death, or freeze to death, or boil to death or will we be killed by burglars? I don't know why we go on living. I don't know why we go on living at all. It's easier being dead.

She flings her arms on the table and buries her head in them. In each of the succeeding speeches she flings her head up—and sometimes her hands—then quickly buries her head again.

MRS. ANTROBUS:

The same thing! Always throwing up the sponge, Sabina. Always announcing your own death. But give you a new hat—or a plate of ice cream—or a ticket to the movies, and you want to live forever.

SABINA:

You don't care whether we live or die; all you care about is those children. If it would be any benefit to them you'd be glad to see us all stretched out dead.

MRS. ANTROBUS:

Well, maybe I would.

SABINA:

And what do they care about? Themselves—that's all they care about.

Shrilly.

They make fun of you behind your back. Don't tell me: they're ashamed of you. Half the time, they pretend they're someone else's children. Little thanks you get from them.

MRS. ANTROBUS:

I'm not asking for any thanks.

SABINA:

And Mr. Antrobus—you don't understand *him*. All that

work he does—trying to discover the alphabet and the multiplication table. Whenever he tries to learn anything, you fight against it.

MRS. ANTROBUS:

Oh, Sabina, I know you.
When Mr. Antrobus raped you home from your Sabine hills, he did it to insult me.
He did it for your pretty face, and to insult me.
You were the new wife, weren't you?
For a year or two you lay on your bed all day and polished the nails on your hands and feet.
You made puffballs of the combings of your hair and you blew them up to the ceiling.
And I washed your underclothes and I made you chicken broths.
I bore children and between my very groans I stirred the cream that you'd put on your face.
But I knew you wouldn't last.
You didn't last.

SABINA:

But it was I who encouraged Mr. Antrobus to make the alphabet. I'm sorry to say it, Mrs. Antrobus, but you're not a beautiful woman, and you can never know what a man could do if he tried. It's girls like I who inspire the multiplication table.
I'm sorry to say it, but you're not a beautiful woman, Mrs. Antrobus, and that's the God's truth.

MRS. ANTROBUS:

And you didn't last—you sank to the kitchen. And what do you do there? *You let the fire go out!*
No wonder to you it seems easier being dead.
Reading and writing and counting on your fingers is all very well in their way, —but I keep the home going.
—There's that dinosaur on the front lawn again. —Shoo! Go away. Go away.

The baby DINOSAUR *puts his head in the window.*

DINOSAUR:

It's cold.

MRS. ANTROBUS:

You go around to the back of the house where you belong.

DINOSAUR:

It's cold.

The DINOSAUR *disappears.* MRS. ANTROBUS *goes calmly out.* SABINA *slowly raises her head and speaks to the audience. The central portion of the center wall rises, pauses, and disappears into the loft.*

SABINA:

Now that you audience are listening to this, too, I understand it a little better.
I wish eleven o'clock were here; I don't want to be dragged through this whole play again.

The TELEGRAPH BOY *is seen entering along the back wall of the stage from the right. She catches sight of him and calls.*

Mrs. Antrobus! Mrs. Antrobus! Help! There's a strange man coming to the house. He's coming up the walk, help!

Enter MRS. ANTROBUS *in alarm, but efficient.*

MRS. ANTROBUS:

Help me quick!

They barricade the door by piling the furniture against it.

Who is it? What do you want?

TELEGRAPH BOY:

A telegram for Mrs. Antrobus from Mr. Antrobus in the city.

SABINA:

Are you sure, are you sure? Maybe it's just a trap!

MRS. ANTROBUS:

I know his voice, Sabina. We can open the door.

Enter the TELEGRAPH BOY, *12 years old, in uniform. The* DINOSAUR *and* MAMMOTH *slip by him into the room and settle down front right.*

I'm sorry we kept you waiting. We have to be careful, you know.

To the animals.

Hm! . . . Will you be quiet?

They nod.

Have you had your supper?

They nod.

Are you *ready* to come in?

They nod.

Young man, have you any fire with you? Then light the grate, will you?

He nods, produces something like a briquet, and kneels by the imagined fireplace, footlights center. Pause.

What are people saying about this cold weather?

He makes a doubtful shrug with his shoulders.

Sabina, take this stick and go and light the stove.

SABINA:

Like I told you, Mrs. Antrobus; two weeks. That's the law. I hope that's perfectly clear.

Exit.

MRS. ANTROBUS:

What about this cold weather?

TELEGRAPH BOY:

Lowered eyes.

Of course, I don't know anything . . . but they say there's a wall of ice moving down from the north, that's what they say. We can't get Boston by telegraph, and they're burning pianos in Hartford.

. . . It moves everything in front of it, churches and post offices and city halls.

I live in Brooklyn myself.

MRS. ANTROBUS:

What are people doing about it?

TELEGRAPH BOY:

Well . . . uh . . . Talking, mostly.

Or just what you'd do a day in February.
There are some that are trying to go south and the roads are crowded; but you can't take old people and children very far in a cold like this.

MRS. ANTROBUS:

—What's this telegram you have for me?

TELEGRAPH BOY:

Fingertips to his forehead.

If you wait just a minute; I've got to remember it.

The animals have left their corner and are nosing him. Presently they take places on either side of him, leaning against his hips, like heraldic beasts.

This telegram was flashed from Murray Hill to University Heights! And then by puffs of smoke from University Heights to Staten Island.
And then by lantern from Staten Island to Plainfield, New Jersey. What hath God wrought!

He clears his throat.

"To Mrs. Antrobus, Excelsior, New Jersey:
My dear wife, will be an hour late. Busy day at the office. Don't worry the children about the cold just keep them warm burn everything except Shakespeare."

Pause.

MRS. ANTROBUS:

Men! —He knows I'd burn ten Shakespeares to prevent a child of mine from having one cold in the head. What does it say next?

Enter SABINA.

TELEGRAPH BOY:

"Have made great discoveries today have separated em from en."

SABINA:

I know what that is, that's the alphabet, yes it is. Mr. Antrobus is just the cleverest man. Why, when the alphabet's finished, we'll be able to tell the future and everything.

TELEGRAPH BOY:

Then listen to this: "Ten tens make a hundred semicolon consequences far-reaching."

Watches for effect.

MRS. ANTROBUS:

The earth's turning to ice, and all he can do is to make up new numbers.

TELEGRAPH BOY:

Well, Mrs. Antrobus, like the head man at our office said: a few more discoveries like that and we'll be worth freezing.

MRS. ANTROBUS:

What does he say next?

TELEGRAPH BOY:

I . . . I can't do this last part very well.

He clears his throat and sings.

"Happy w'dding ann'vers'ry to you, Happy ann'vers'ry to you—"

The animals begin to howl soulfully; SABINA *screams with pleasure.*

MRS. ANTROBUS:

Dolly! Frederick! Be quiet.

TELEGRAPH BOY:

Above the din.

"Happy w'dding ann'vers'ry, dear Eva; happy w'dding ann'vers'ry to you."

MRS. ANTROBUS:

Is that in the telegram? Are they singing telegrams now?

He nods.

The earth's getting so silly no wonder the sun turns cold.

SABINA:

Mrs. Antrobus, I want to take back the notice I gave you. Mrs. Antrobus, I don't want to leave a house that gets such interesting telegrams and I'm sorry for anything I said. I really am.

MRS. ANTROBUS:

Young man, I'd like to give you something for all this trouble; Mr. Antrobus isn't home yet and I have no money and no food in the house—

TELEGRAPH BOY:

Mrs. Antrobus . . . I don't like to . . . appear to . . . ask for anything, but . . .

MRS. ANTROBUS:

What is it you'd like?

TELEGRAPH BOY:

Do you happen to have an old needle you could spare? My wife just sits home all day thinking about needles.

SABINA:

Shrilly.

We only got two in the house. Mrs. Antrobus, you know we only got two in the house.

MRS. ANTROBUS:

After a look at SABINA, *taking a needle from her collar.*

Why, yes, I can spare this.

TELEGRAPH BOY:

Lowered eyes.

Thank you, Mrs. Antrobus. Mrs. Antrobus, can I ask you something else? I have two sons of my own; if the cold gets worse, what should I do?

SABINA:

I think we'll all perish, that's what I think. Cold like this in August is just the end of the whole world.

Silence.

MRS. ANTROBUS:

I don't know. After all, what does one do about anything? Just keep as warm as you can. And don't let your wife and children see that you're worried.

TELEGRAPH BOY:

Yes. . . . Thank you, Mrs. Antrobus. Well, I'd better be going. —Oh, I forgot! There's one more sentence in the telegram.
"Three cheers have invented the wheel."

MRS. ANTROBUS:

A wheel? What's a wheel?

TELEGRAPH BOY:

I don't know. That's what it said. The sign for it is like this.
Well, good-by.

The women see him to the door, with good-bys and injunctions to keep warm.

SABINA:

Apron to her eyes, wailing.

Mrs. Antrobus, it looks to me like all the nice men in the world are already married; I don't know why that is.

Exit.

MRS. ANTROBUS:

Thoughtful; to the animals.

Do you ever remember hearing tell of any cold like this in August?

The animals shake their heads.

From your grandmothers or anyone?

They shake their heads.

Have you any suggestions?

They shake their heads.

She pulls her shawl around, goes to the front door and, opening it an inch, calls.

HENRY. GLADYS. CHILDREN. Come right in and get warm. No, no, when Mama says a thing she means it. Henry! HENRY. Put down that stone. You know what happened last time.

Shriek.

HENRY! Put down that stone!

Gladys! Put down your dress!! Try and be a lady.

The children bound in and dash to the fire. They take off their winter things and leave them in heaps on the floor.

GLADYS:

Mama, I'm hungry. Mama, why is it so cold?

HENRY:

At the same time.

Mama, why doesn't it snow? Mama, when's supper ready? Maybe it'll snow and we can make snowballs.

GLADYS:

Mama, it's so cold that in one more minute I just couldn't of stood it.

MRS. ANTROBUS:

Settle down, both of you, I want to talk to you.

She draws up a hassock and sits front center over the orchestra pit before the imaginary fire. The children stretch out on the floor, leaning against her lap. Tableau by Raphael. The animals edge up and complete the triangle.

It's just a cold spell of some kind. Now listen to what I'm saying:
When your father comes home I want you to be extra quiet. He's had a hard day at the office and I don't know but what he may have one of his moods.
I just got a telegram from him very happy and excited, and you know what that means. Your father's temper's uneven; I guess you know that.

Shriek.

Henry! Henry!
Why—why can't you remember to keep your hair down over your forehead? You must keep that scar covered up. Don't you know that when your father sees it he loses all control over himself? He goes crazy. He wants to die.

After a moment's despair she collects herself decisively, wets the hem of her apron in her mouth and starts polishing his forehead vigorously.

Lift your head up. Stop squirming. Blessed me, sometimes I think that it's going away—and then there it is: just as red as ever.

HENRY:

Mama, today at school two teachers forgot and called me by my old name. They forgot, Mama. You'd better write another letter to the principal, so that he'll tell them I've changed my name. Right out in class they called me: Cain.

MRS. ANTROBUS:

Putting her hand on his mouth, too late; hoarsely.

Don't say it.

Polishing feverishly.

If you're good they'll forget it. Henry, you didn't hit any-one . . . today, did you?

HENRY:

Oh . . . no-o-o!

MRS. ANTROBUS:

Still working, not looking at GLADYS.

And, Gladys, I want you to be especially nice to your father tonight. You know what he calls you when you're good—his little angel, his little star. Keep your dress down like a little lady. And keep your voice nice and low. Gladys Antrobus!! What's that red stuff you have on your face?

Slaps her.

You're a filthy detestable child!

Rises in real, though temporary, repudiation and despair.

Get away from me, both of you! I wish I'd never seen sight or sound of you. Let the cold come! I can't stand it. I don't want to go on.

She walks away.

GLADYS:

Weeping.

All the girls at school do, Mama.

MRS. ANTROBUS:

Shrieking.

I'm through with you, that's all! —Sabina! Sabina! — Don't you know your father'd go crazy if he saw that paint on your face? Don't you know your father thinks you're perfect? Don't you know he couldn't live if he didn't think you were perfect? —Sabina!

Enter SABINA.

SABINA:

Yes, Mrs. Antrobus!

MRS. ANTROBUS:

Take this girl out into the kitchen and wash her face with the scrubbing brush.

MR. ANTROBUS:

Outside, roaring.

"I've been working on the railroad, all the livelong day . . ." etc.

The animals start running around in circles, bellowing. SABINA *rushes to the window.*

MRS. ANTROBUS:

Sabina, what's that noise outside?

SABINA:

Oh, it's a drunken tramp. It's a giant, Mrs. Antrobus. We'll all be killed in our beds, I know it!

MRS. ANTROBUS:

Help me quick. Quick. Everybody.

Again they stack all the furniture against the door. MR. ANTROBUS *pounds and bellows.*

Who is it? What do you want? —Sabina, have you any boiling water ready? —Who is it?

MR. ANTROBUS:

Broken-down camel of a pig's snout, open this door.

MRS. ANTROBUS:

God be praised! It's your father. —Just a minute, George! —Sabina, clear the door, quick. Gladys, come here while I clean your nasty face!

MR. ANTROBUS:

She-bitch of a goat's gizzard, I'll break every bone in your body. Let me in or I'll tear the whole house down.

MRS. ANTROBUS:

Just a minute, George, something's the matter with the lock.

MR. ANTROBUS:

Open the door or I'll tear your livers out. I'll smash your brains on the ceiling, and Devil take the hindmost.

MRS. ANTROBUS:

Now, you can open the door, Sabina. I'm ready.

The door is flung open. Silence. MR. ANTROBUS*—face of a Keystone Comedy Cop—stands there in fur cap and blanket. His arms are full of parcels, including a large stone wheel with a center in it. One hand carries a railroad man's lantern. Suddenly he bursts into joyous roar.*

MR. ANTROBUS:

Well, how's the whole crooked family?

Relief. Laughter. Tears. Jumping up and down. Animals cavorting. MR. ANTROBUS *throws the parcels on the ground. Hurls his cap and blanket after them. Heroic embraces. Melee of humans and animals,* SABINA *included.*

I'll be scalded and tarred if a man can't get a little welcome when he comes home. Well, Maggie, you old gunny sack, how's the broken-down old weather hen? —Sabina, old fishbait, old skunkpot. —And the children—how've the little smellers been?

GLADYS:

Papa, Papa, Papa, Papa, Papa.

MR. ANTROBUS:

How've they been, Maggie?

MRS. ANTROBUS:

Well, I must say, they've been as good as gold. I haven't had to raise my voice once. I don't know what's the matter with them.

MR. ANTROBUS:

Kneeling before GLADYS.

Papa's little weasel, eh? —Sabina, there's some food for you. —Papa's little gopher?

GLADYS:

Her arm around his neck.

Papa, you're always teasing me.

MR. ANTROBUS:

And Henry? Nothing rash today, I hope. Nothing rash?

HENRY:

No, Papa.

MR. ANTROBUS:

Roaring.

Well that's good, that's good— I'll bet Sabina let the fire go out.

SABINA:

Mr. Antrobus, I've given my notice. I'm leaving two weeks from today. I'm sorry, but I'm leaving.

MR. ANTROBUS:

Roar.

Well, if you leave now you'll freeze to death, so go and cook the dinner.

SABINA:

Two weeks, that's the law.

Exit.

MR. ANTROBUS:

Did you get my telegram?

MRS. ANTROBUS:

Yes. —What's a wheel?

He indicates the wheel with a glance. HENRY *is rolling it around the floor. Rapid, hoarse interchange:* MRS. ANTROBUS: *What does this cold weather mean? It's below freezing.* MR. ANTROBUS: *Not before the children!* MRS. ANTROBUS: *Shouldn't we do something about it? —start off, move?* MR. ANTROBUS: *Not before the children!!! He gives* HENRY *a sharp slap.*

HENRY:

Papa, you hit me!

MR. ANTROBUS:

Well, remember it. That's to make you remember today. Today. The day the alphabet's finished; and the day that we *saw* the hundred—the hundred, the hundred, the hundred, the hundred, the hundred—there's no end to 'em.
I've had a day at the office!
Take a look at that wheel, Maggie—when I've got that to rights: you'll see a sight.
There's a reward there for all the walking you've done.

MRS. ANTROBUS:

How do you mean?

MR. ANTROBUS:

On the hassock looking into the fire; with awe.
Maggie, we've reached the top of the wave. There's not much more to be done. We're there!

MRS. ANTROBUS:

Cutting across his mood sharply.
And the ice?

MR. ANTROBUS:

The ice!

HENRY:

Playing with the wheel.

Papa, you could put a chair on this.

MR. ANTROBUS:

Broodingly.

Ye-e-s, any booby can fool with it now, —but I thought of it first.

MRS. ANTROBUS:

Children, go out in the kitchen. I want to talk to your father alone.

The children go out.

MR. ANTROBUS *has moved to his chair up left. He takes the goldfish bowl on his lap; pulls the canary cage down to the level of his face. Both the animals put their paws up on the arm of his chair.* MRS. ANTROBUS *faces him across the room, like a judge.*

Well?

MR. ANTROBUS:

Shortly.

It's cold. —How things been, eh? Keck, keck, keck. —And you, Millicent?

MRS. ANTROBUS:

I know it's cold.

MR. ANTROBUS:

To the canary.

No spilling of sunflower seed, eh? No singing after lights-out, y'know what I mean?

MRS. ANTROBUS:

You can try and prevent us freezing to death, can't you? You can do something? We can start moving. Or we can go on the animals' backs?

MR. ANTROBUS:

The best thing about animals is that they don't talk much.

MAMMOTH:

It's cold.

MR. ANTROBUS:

Eh, eh, eh! Watch that!—

—By midnight we'd turn to ice. The roads are full of people now who can scarcely lift a foot from the ground. The grass out in front is like iron—which reminds me, I have another needle for you. —The people up north—where are they? Frozen . . . crushed. . . .

MRS. ANTROBUS:

Is that what's going to happen to us? —Will you answer me?

MR. ANTROBUS:

I don't know. I don't know anything. Some say that the

ice is going slower. Some say that it's stopped. The sun's growing cold. What can I do about that? Nothing we can do but burn everything in the house, and the fenceposts and the barn. Keep the fire going. When we have no more fire, we die.

MRS. ANTROBUS:

Well, why didn't you say so in the first place?

MRS. ANTROBUS *is about to march off when she catches sight of two* REFUGEES, *men, who have appeared against the back wall of the theatre and who are soon joined by others.*

REFUGEES:

Mr. Antrobus! Mr. Antrobus! Mr. An-nn-tro-bus!

MRS. ANTROBUS:

Who's that? Who's that calling you?

MR. ANTROBUS:

Clearing his throat guiltily.

Hm—let me see.

Two REFUGEES *come up to the window.*

REFUGEE:

Could we warm our hands for a moment, Mr. Antrobus? It's very cold, Mr. Antrobus.

ANOTHER REFUGEE:

Mr. Antrobus, I wonder if you have a piece of bread or something that you could spare.

Silence. They wait humbly. MRS. ANTROBUS *stands rooted to the spot. Suddenly a knock at the door, then another hand knocking in short rapid blows.*

MRS. ANTROBUS:

Who are these people? Why, they're all over the front yard. What have they come *here* for?

Enter SABINA.

SABINA:

Mrs. Antrobus! There are some tramps knocking at the back door.

MRS. ANTROBUS:

George, tell these people to go away. Tell them to move right along. I'll go and send them away from the back door. Sabina, come with me.

She goes out energetically.

MR. ANTROBUS:

Sabina! Stay here! I have something to say to you.

He goes to the door and opens it a crack and talks through it.

Ladies and gentlemen! I'll have to ask you to wait a few minutes longer. It'll be all right. . . . While you're waiting you might each one pull up a stake of the fence. We'll need them all for the fireplace. There'll be coffee and sandwiches in a moment.

SABINA *looks out door over his shoulder and suddenly extends her arm pointing, with a scream.*

SABINA:

Mr. Antrobus, what's that?? —that big white thing? Mr. Antrobus, it's ICE. It's ICE!!

MR. ANTROBUS:

Sabina, I want you to go in the kitchen and make a lot of coffee. Make a whole pail full.

SABINA:

Pail full!!

MR. ANTROBUS:

With gesture.

And sandwiches . . . piles of them . . . like this.

SABINA:

Mr. An . . . !!

Suddenly she drops the play, and says in her own person as MISS SOMERSET, *with surprise.*

Oh, *I* see what this part of the play means now! This means refugees.

She starts to cross to the proscenium.

Oh, I don't like it. I don't like it.

She leans against the proscenium and bursts into tears.

MR. ANTROBUS:

Miss Somerset!

STAGE MANAGER:

Offstage.

Miss Somerset!

SABINA:

Energetically, to the audience.

Ladies and gentlemen! Don't take this play serious. The world's not coming to an end. You know it's not. People exaggerate! Most people really have enough to eat and a roof over their heads. Nobody actually starves—you can always eat grass or something. That ice business—why, it was a long, long time ago. Besides, they were only savages. Savages don't love their families—not like we do.

MR. ANTROBUS *and* STAGE MANAGER:

Miss Somerset!!

There is renewed knocking at the door.

SABINA:

All right. I'll say the lines, but I won't think about the play.

Enter MRS. ANTROBUS.

SABINA *delivers a parting thrust at the audience.*

And I advise *you* not to think about the play, either.

Exit SABINA.

MRS. ANTROBUS:

George, these tramps say that you asked them to come to the house. What does this mean?

Knocking at the door.

MR. ANTROBUS:

Just . . . uh . . . There are a few friends, Maggie, I met on the road. Real nice, real useful people. . . .

MRS. ANTROBUS:

Back to the door.

Now, don't you ask them in!
George Antrobus, not another soul comes in here over my dead body.

MR. ANTROBUS:

Maggie, there's a doctor there. Never hurts to have a good doctor in the house. We've lost a peck of children, one way and another. You can never tell when a child's throat will get stopped up. What you and I have seen—!!!

He puts his fingers on his throat, and imitates diphtheria.

MRS. ANTROBUS:

Well, just one person then, the doctor. The others can go right along the road.

MR. ANTROBUS:

Maggie, there's an old man, particular friend of mine—

MRS. ANTROBUS:

I won't listen to you—

MR. ANTROBUS:

It was he that really started off the ABC's.

MRS. ANTROBUS:

I don't care if he perishes. We can do without reading or writing. We can't do without food.

MR. ANTROBUS:

Then let the ice come!! Drink your coffee!! I don't want any coffee if I can't drink it with some good people.

MRS. ANTROBUS:

Stop shouting. Who else is there trying to push us off the cliff?

MR. ANTROBUS:

Well, there's the man . . . who makes all the laws. Judge Moses!

MRS. ANTROBUS:

Judges can't help us now.

MR. ANTROBUS:

And if the ice melts? . . . and if we pull through? Have you and I been able to bring up Henry? What have we done?

MRS. ANTROBUS:

Who are those old women?

MR. ANTROBUS:

Coughs.

Up in town there are nine sisters. There are three or four of them here. They're sort of music teachers . . . and one of them recites and one of them—

MRS. ANTROBUS:

That's the end. A singing troupe! Well, take your choice, live or die. Starve your own children before your face.

MR. ANTROBUS:

Gently.

These people don't take much. They're used to starving. They'll sleep on the floor.

Besides, Maggie, listen: no, listen:

Who've we got in the house but Sabina? Sabina's always afraid the worst will happen. Whose spirits can she keep up? Maggie, these people never give up. They think they'll live and work forever.

MRS. ANTROBUS:

Walks slowly to the middle of the room.

All right, let them in. Let them in. You're master here.

Softly.

—But these animals must go. Enough's enough. They'll soon be big enough to push the walls down, anyway. Take them away.

MR. ANTROBUS:

Sadly.

All right. The dinosaur and mammoth—! Come on, baby, come on Frederick. Come for a walk. That's a good little fellow.

DINOSAUR:

It's cold.

MR. ANTROBUS:

Yes, nice cold fresh air. Bracing.

He holds the door open and the animals go out. He beckons to his friends. The REFUGEES *are typical elderly out-of-works from the streets of New York today.* JUDGE MOSES *wears a skullcap.* HOMER *is a blind beggar with a guitar. The seedy crowd shuffles in and waits humbly and expectantly.* MR. ANTROBUS *introduces them to his wife who bows to each with a stately bend of her head.*

Make yourself at home. Maggie, this is the doctor . . . m . . . Coffee'll be here in a minute. . . . Professor, this is my wife. . . . And: . . . Judge . . . Maggie, you know the judge.

An old blind man with a guitar.

Maggie, you know . . . you know Homer? —Come right in, Judge.

Miss Muse—are some of your sisters here? Come right in. . . . Miss E. Muse, Miss T. Muse, Miss M. Muse.

MRS. ANTROBUS:

Pleased to meet you.

Just . . . make yourself comfortable. Supper'll be ready in a minute.

She goes out, abruptly.

MR. ANTROBUS:

Make yourself at home, friends. I'll be right back.

He goes out.

The REFUGEES *stare about them in awe. Presently several voices start whispering "Homer! Homer!" All take it up.* HOMER *strikes a chord or two on his guitar, then starts to speak.*

HOMER:

Μῆνιν ἄειδε, θεὰ, Πηληϊάδεω Ἀχιλῆος,
οὐλομένην, ἣ μυρί' Ἀχαιοῖς ἄλγε' ἔθηκεν,
πολλὰς δ' ἰφθίμους ψυχὰς—

Homer's face shows he is lost in thought and memory and the words die away on his lips. The REFUGEES *likewise nod in dreamy recollection. Soon the whisper "Moses, Moses!" goes around. An aged Jew parts his beard and recites dramatically.*

MOSES:

בְּרֵאשִׁית בָּרָא אֱלֹהִים אֵת הַשָּׁמַיִם וְאֵת הָאָרֶץ׃ וְהָאָרֶץ הָיְתָה תֹהוּ
וָבֹהוּ וְחֹשֶׁךְ עַל־פְּנֵי תְהוֹם וְרוּחַ אֱלֹהִים מְרַחֶפֶת עַל־פְּנֵי הַמָּיִם׃

The same dying away of the words takes place, and on the part of the REFUGEES *the same retreat into recollection. Some of them murmur "Yes, yes."*
The mood is broken by the abrupt entrance of MR. *and* MRS. ANTROBUS *and* SABINA *bearing platters of sandwiches and a pail of coffee.* SABINA *stops and stares at the guests.*

MR. ANTROBUS:

Sabina, pass the sandwiches.

SABINA:

I thought I was working in a respectable house that had respectable guests. I'm giving my notice, Mr. Antrobus: two weeks, that's the law.

MR. ANTROBUS:

Sabina! Pass the sandwiches.

SABINA:

Two weeks, that's the law.

MR. ANTROBUS:

There's the law. That's Moses.

SABINA:

Stares.

The Ten Commandments— FAUGH!!

To audience.

That's the worst line I've ever had to say on any stage.

MR. ANTROBUS:

I think the best thing to do is just not to stand on ceremony, but pass the sandwiches around from left to right. —Judge, help yourself to one of these.

MRS. ANTROBUS:

The roads are crowded, I hear?

THE GUESTS:

All talking at once.

Oh, ma'am, you can't imagine. . . . You can hardly put one foot before you . . . people are trampling one another.

Sudden silence.

MRS. ANTROBUS:

Well, you know what I think it is— I think it's sunspots!

THE GUESTS:

Discreet hubbub.

Oh, you're right, Mrs. Antrobus . . . that's what it is. . . . That's what I was saying the other day.

Sudden silence.

MR. ANTROBUS:

Well, I don't believe the whole world's going to turn to ice.

All eyes are fixed on him, waiting.

I can't believe it. Judge! Have we worked for nothing? Professor! Have we just failed in the whole thing?

MRS. ANTROBUS:

It is certainly very strange—well, fortunately on both sides of the family we come of very hearty stock. —Doctor, I want you to meet my children. They're eating their supper now. And of course I want them to meet you.

MISS M. MUSE:

How many children have you, Mrs. Antrobus?

MRS. ANTROBUS:

I have two, —a boy and a girl.

MOSES:

Softly.

I understood you had two sons, Mrs. Antrobus.

MRS. ANTROBUS *in blind suffering; she walks toward the footlights.*

MRS. ANTROBUS:

In a low voice.

Abel, Abel, my son, my son, Abel, my son, Abel, Abel, my son.

The REFUGEES *move with a few steps toward her as though in comfort, murmuring words in Greek, Hebrew, German, etc.*
A piercing shriek from the kitchen—Sabina's voice.
All heads turn.

MR. ANTROBUS:

What's that?

SABINA *enters, bursting with indignation, pulling on her gloves.*

SABINA:

Mr. Antrobus—that son of yours, that boy Henry Antrobus—I don't stay in this house another moment! —He's not fit to live among respectable folks and that's a fact.

MRS. ANTROBUS:

Don't say another word, Sabina. I'll be right back.

Without waiting for an answer she goes past her into the kitchen.

SABINA:

Mr. Antrobus, Henry has thrown a stone again and if he hasn't killed the boy that lives next door, I'm very much mistaken. He finished his supper and went out to play;

and I heard such a fight; and then I saw it. I saw it with my own eyes. And it looked to me like stark murder.

MRS. ANTROBUS *appears at the kitchen door, shielding* HENRY *who follows her. When she steps aside, we see on Henry's forehead a large ochre and scarlet scar in the shape of a C.* MR. ANTROBUS *starts toward him.*

A pause.

HENRY:

Under his breath.

He was going to take the wheel away from me. He started to throw a stone at me first.

MRS. ANTROBUS:

George, it was just a boyish impulse. Remember how young he is.

Louder, in an urgent wail.

George, he's only four thousand years old.

SABINA:

And everything was going along so nicely!

Silence. MR. ANTROBUS *goes back to the fireplace.*

MR. ANTROBUS:

Put out the fire! Put out all the fires.

Violently.

No wonder the sun grows cold.

He starts stamping on the fireplace.

MRS. ANTROBUS:

Doctor! Judge! Help me! —George, have you lost your mind?

MR. ANTROBUS:

There is no mind. We'll not try to live.

To the guests.

Give it up. Give up trying.

MRS. ANTROBUS *seizes him.*

SABINA:

Mr. Antrobus! I'm downright ashamed of you.

MRS. ANTROBUS:

George, have some more coffee. —Gladys! Where's Gladys gone?

GLADYS *steps in, frightened.*

GLADYS:

Here I am, Mama.

MRS. ANTROBUS:

Go upstairs and bring your father's slippers. How could you forget a thing like that, when you know how tired he is?

MR. ANTROBUS *sits in his chair. He covers his face with his hands.* MRS. ANTROBUS *turns to the* REFUGEES.

Can't some of you sing? It's your business in life to sing, isn't it? Sabina!

Several of the women clear their throats tentatively, and with frightened faces gather around Homer's guitar. He establishes a few chords. Almost inaudibly they start singing, led by SABINA, *"Jingle Bells."*

MRS. ANTROBUS *continues to* MR. ANTROBUS *in a low voice, while taking off his shoes.*

George, remember all the other times. When the volcanoes came right up in the front yard.
And the time the grasshoppers ate every single leaf and blade of grass, and all the grain and spinach you'd grown with your own hands. And the summer there were earthquakes every night.

MR. ANTROBUS:

Henry! Henry!

Puts his hand on his forehead.

Myself. All of us, we're covered with blood.

MRS. ANTROBUS:

Then remember all the times you were pleased with him and when you were proud of yourself. —Henry! Henry! Come here and recite to your father the multiplication table that you do so nicely.

HENRY *kneels on one knee beside his father and starts whispering the multiplication table.*

HENRY:

Finally.

Two times six is twelve; three times six is eighteen—I don't think I know the sixes.

Enter GLADYS *with the slippers.* MRS. ANTROBUS *makes stern gestures to her: Go in there and do your best. The guests are now singing "Tenting Tonight."*

GLADYS:

Putting slippers on his feet.

Papa . . . Papa . . . I was very good in school today. Miss

Conover said right out in class that if all the girls had as good manners as Gladys Antrobus, that the world would be a very different place to live in.

MRS. ANTROBUS:

You recited a piece at assembly, didn't you? Recite it to your father.

GLADYS:

Papa, do you want to hear what I recited in class?

Fierce directorial glance from her mother.

"THE STAR" by Henry Wadsworth LONGFELLOW.

MRS. ANTROBUS:

Wait!!! The fire's going out. There isn't enough wood! Henry, go upstairs and bring down the chairs and start breaking up the beds.

Exit HENRY. *The singers return to "Jingle Bells," still very softly.*

GLADYS:

Look, Papa, here's my report card. Lookit. Conduct A! Look, Papa. Papa, do you want to hear "The Star," by Henry Wadsworth Longfellow? Papa, you're not mad at me, are you? —I know it'll get warmer. Soon it'll be just like spring, and we can go to a picnic at the Hibernian Picnic Grounds like you always like to do, don't you remember? Papa, just look at me once.

Enter HENRY *with some chairs.*

MR. ANTROBUS:

You recited in assembly, did you?

She nods eagerly.

You didn't forget it?

GLADYS:

No!!! I was perfect.

Pause. Then MR. ANTROBUS *rises, goes to the front door and opens it. The* REFUGEES *draw back timidly; the song stops; he peers out of the door, then closes it.*

MR. ANTROBUS:

With decision, suddenly.

Build up the fire. It's cold. Build up the fire. We'll do what we can. Sabina, get some more wood. Come around the fire, everybody. At least the young ones may pull through. Henry, have you eaten something?

HENRY:

Yes, Papa.

MR. ANTROBUS:

Gladys, have you had some supper?

GLADYS:

I ate in the kitchen, Papa.

MR. ANTROBUS:

If you do come through this—what'll you be able to do? What do you know? Henry, did you take a good look at that wheel?

HENRY:

Yes, Papa.

MR. ANTROBUS:

Sitting down in his chair.
Six times two are—

HENRY:

—twelve; six times three are eighteen; six times four are—Papa, it's hot and cold. It makes my head all funny. It makes me sleepy.

MR. ANTROBUS:

Gives him a cuff.
Wake up. I don't care if your head is sleepy. Six times four are twenty-four. Six times five are—

HENRY:

Thirty. Papa!

MR. ANTROBUS:

Maggie, put something into Gladys' head on the chance she can use it.

MRS. ANTROBUS:

What do you mean, George?

MR. ANTROBUS:

Six times six are thirty-six.
Teach her the beginning of the Bible.

GLADYS:

But, Mama, it's so cold and close.

HENRY *has all but drowsed off. His father slaps him sharply and the lesson goes on.*

MRS. ANTROBUS:

"In the beginning God created the heavens and the earth; and the earth was waste and void; and the darkness was upon the face of the deep—"

The singing starts up again louder. SABINA *has returned with wood. After placing wood on the fireplace, she comes down to the footlights and addresses the audience.*

SABINA:

Will you please start handing up your chairs? We'll need everything for this fire. Save the human race. —Ushers, will you pass the chairs up here? Thank you.

HENRY:

Six times nine are fifty-four; six times ten are sixty.

In the back of the auditorium the sound of chairs being ripped up can be heard. USHERS *rush down the aisles with chairs and hand them over.*

GLADYS:

"And God called the light Day and the darkness he called Night."

SABINA:

Pass up your chairs, everybody. Save the human race.

CURTAIN

Act Two

Toward the end of the intermission, though with the houselights still up, lantern slide projections begin to appear on the curtain. Timetables for trains leaving Pennsylvania Station for Atlantic City. Advertisements of Atlantic City hotels, drugstores, churches, rug merchants, fortune tellers, bingo parlors.

When the houselights go down, the voice of an ANNOUNCER *is heard.*

ANNOUNCER:

The Management now brings you the News Events of the World. Atlantic City, New Jersey:

Projection of a chrome postcard of the waterfront, trimmed in mica with the legend: FUN AT THE BEACH.

This great convention city is playing host this week to the anniversary convocation of that great fraternal order, — the Ancient and Honorable Order of Mammals, Subdivision Humans. This great fraternal, militant, and burial society is celebrating on the Boardwalk, ladies and gentlemen, its six hundred thousandth Annual Convention.

It has just elected its president for the ensuing term—

Projection of MR. *and* MRS. ANTROBUS *posed as they will be shown a few moments later.*

Mr. George Antrobus of Excelsior, New Jersey. We show you President Antrobus and his gracious and charming wife, every inch a mammal. Mr. Antrobus has had a long and chequered career. Credit has been paid to him for many useful enterprises including the introduction of the lever, of the wheel, and the brewing of beer. Credit has been also extended to President Antrobus' gracious and charming wife for many practical suggestions, including the hem, the gore, and the gusset; and the novelty of the year, —frying in oil. Before we show you Mr. Antrobus accepting the nomination, we have an important announcement to make. As many of you know, this great celebration of the Order of the Mammals has received delegations from the other rival Orders, —or shall we say: esteemed concurrent Orders: the WINGS, the FINS, the SHELLS, and so on. These Orders are holding their conventions also, in various parts of the world, and have sent representatives to our own, two of a kind.

Later in the day we will show you President Antrobus broadcasting his words of greeting and congratulation to the collected assemblies of the whole natural world.

Ladies and Gentlemen! We give you President Antrobus!

The screen becomes a transparency. MR. ANTROBUS *stands beside a pedestal;* MRS. ANTROBUS *is seated wearing a corsage of orchids.* MR. ANTROBUS *wears an untidy Prince Albert; spats; from a red rosette in his buttonhole hangs a fine long purple ribbon of honor. He wears a gay lodge hat—something between a fez and a legionnaire's cap.*

MR. ANTROBUS:

Fellow mammals, fellow vertebrates, fellow humans, I thank you. Little did my dear parents think, —when they told me to stand on my own two feet, —that I'd arrive at this place.

My friends, we have come a long way.
During this week of happy celebration it is perhaps not fitting that we dwell on some of the difficult times we have been through. The dinosaur is extinct—

Applause.

—the ice has retreated; and the common cold is being pursued by every means within our power.

MRS. ANTROBUS *sneezes, laughs prettily, and murmurs:* "*I beg your pardon.*"

In our memorial service yesterday we did honor to all our friends and relatives who are no longer with us, by reason of cold, earthquakes, plagues, and . . . and . . .

Coughs.

differences of opinion.
As our Bishop so ably said . . . uh . . . so ably said . . .

MRS. ANTROBUS:

Closed lips.

Gone, but not forgotten.

MR. ANTROBUS:

"They are gone, but not forgotten."
I think I can say, I think I can prophesy with complete . . . uh . . . with complete . . .

MRS. ANTROBUS:

Confidence.

MR. ANTROBUS:

Thank you, my dear— With complete lack of confidence, that a new day of security is about to dawn.

The watchword of the closing year was: Work. I give you the watchword for the future: Enjoy Yourselves.

MRS. ANTROBUS:

George, sit down!

MR. ANTROBUS:

Before I close, however, I wish to answer one of those unjust and malicious accusations that were brought against me during this last electoral campaign.
Ladies and gentlemen, the charge was made that at various points in my career I leaned toward joining some of the rival Orders— That's a lie.
As I told reporters of the *Atlantic City Herald*, I do not deny that a few months before my birth I hesitated between . . . uh . . . between pinfeathers and gill breathing, —and so did many of us here, —but for the last million years I have been viviparous, hairy, and diaphragmatic.

Applause. Cries of "Good old Antrobus," "The Prince chap!" "Georgie," etc.

ANNOUNCER:

Thank you. Thank you very much, Mr. Antrobus.
Now I know that our visitors will wish to hear a word from that gracious and charming mammal, Mrs. Antrobus, wife and mother— Mrs. Antrobus!

MRS. ANTROBUS *rises, lays her program on her chair, bows, and speaks.*

MRS. ANTROBUS:

Dear friends, I don't really think I should say anything.

After all, it was my husband who was elected and not I. Perhaps, as president of the Women's Auxiliary Bed and Board Society—I had some notes here, oh, yes, here they are: —I should give a short report from some of our committees that have been meeting in this beautiful city.
Perhaps it may interest you to know that it has at last been decided that the tomato is edible. Can you all hear me? The tomato *is* edible.
A delegate from across the sea reports that the thread woven by the silkworm gives a cloth . . . I have a sample of it here . . . can you see it? smooth, elastic. I should say that it's rather attractive, —though personally I prefer less shiny surfaces. Should the windows of a sleeping apartment be open or shut? I know all mothers will follow our debates on this matter with close interest. I am sorry to say that the most expert authorities have not yet decided. It does seem to me that the night air would be bound to be unhealthy for our children, but there are many distinguished authorities on both sides. Well, I could go on talking forever—as Shakespeare says: a woman's work is seldom done; but I think I'd better join my husband in saying thank you, and sit down. Thank you.

She sits down.

ANNOUNCER:

Oh, Mrs. Antrobus!

MRS. ANTROBUS:

Yes?

ANNOUNCER:

We understand that you are about to celebrate a wedding anniversary. I know our listeners would like to extend their felicitations and hear a few words from you on that subject.

MRS. ANTROBUS:

I have been asked by this kind gentleman . . . yes, my friends, this Spring Mr. Antrobus and I will be celebrating our five thousandth wedding anniversary.
I don't know if I speak for my husband, but I can say that, as for me, I regret every moment of it.

Laughter of confusion.

I beg your pardon. What I *mean* to say is that I do not regret one moment of it. I hope none of you catch my cold. We have two children. We've always had two children, though it hasn't always been the same two. But as I say, we have two fine children, and we're very grateful for that. Yes, Mr. Antrobus and I have been married for five thousand years. Each wedding anniversary reminds me of the times when there were no weddings. We had to crusade for marriage. Perhaps there are some women within the sound of my voice who remember that crusade and those struggles; we fought for it, didn't we? We chained ourselves to lampposts and we made disturbances in the Senate—anyway, at last we women got the ring.
A few men helped us, but I must say that most men blocked our way at every step: they said we were unfeminine.
I only bring up these unpleasant memories because I see some signs of backsliding from that great victory.

Oh, my fellow mammals, keep hold of that.
My husband says that the watchword for the year is Enjoy Yourselves. I think that's very open to misunderstanding. My watchword for the year is: Save the Family. It's held together for over five thousand years: Save it! Thank you.

ANNOUNCER:

Thank you, Mrs. Antrobus.

The transparency disappears.

We had hoped to show you the Beauty Contest that took place here today.
President Antrobus, an experienced judge of pretty girls, gave the title of Miss Atlantic City 1942, to Miss Lily Sabina Fairweather, charming hostess of our Boardwalk Bingo Parlor.
Unfortunately, however, our time is up, and I must take you to some views of the Convention City and conveeners, — enjoying themselves.

A burst of music; the curtain rises.

The Boardwalk. The audience is sitting in the ocean.

A handrail of scarlet cord stretches across the front of the stage.

A ramp—also with scarlet handrail—descends to the right corner of the orchestra pit where a great scarlet beach umbrella or a cabana stands. Front and right stage left are benches facing the sea; attached to each bench is a streetlamp.

The only scenery is two cardboard cutouts six feet high, representing shops at the back of the stage. Reading from left to right they are: SALT WATER TAFFY; FORTUNE TELLER; then the blank space; BINGO PARLOR; TURKISH BATH. They have practical doors, that of the Fortune Teller's being hung with bright gypsy curtains.

By the left proscenium and rising from the orchestra pit is the weather signal; it is like the mast of a ship with crossbars. From time to time black disks are hung on it to indicate the storm and hurricane warnings. Two melancholy Negro CHAIR PUSHERS *file by with three empty roller chairs. Throughout the act they traverse the stage in both directions.*

From time to time, CONVEENERS, *dressed like* MR. ANTROBUS, *cross the stage. Some walk sedately by; others engage in inane horseplay. The old gypsy* FORTUNE TELLER *is seated at the door of her shop, smoking a corncob pipe.*

From the Bingo Parlor comes the voice of the BINGO CALLER.

BINGO CALLER:

A-nine; A-nine. C-twenty-six; C-twenty-six. A-four; A-four. B-twelve.

CHORUS:

Backstage.

Bingo!!!

The front of the Bingo Parlor shudders, rises a few feet in the air, and returns to the ground trembling.

FORTUNE TELLER:

Mechanically, to the unconscious back of a passerby, pointing with her pipe.

Bright's disease. Your partner's deceiving you in that Kansas City deal. You'll have six grandchildren. Avoid high places.

She rises and shouts after another.

Cirrhosis of the liver!

SABINA *appears at the door of the Bingo Parlor. She hugs about her a blue raincoat that almost conceals her red bathing suit. She tries to catch the Fortune Teller's attention.*

SABINA:

Ssssst! Esmeralda! Ssssst!

FORTUNE TELLER:

Keck!

SABINA:

Has President Antrobus come along yet?

FORTUNE TELLER:

No, no, no. Get back there. Hide yourself.

SABINA:

I'm afraid I'll miss him. Oh, Esmeralda, if I fail in this, I'll die; I know I'll die. President Antrobus!!! And I'll be his wife! If it's the last thing I'll do, I'll be Mrs. George Antrobus. —Esmeralda, tell me my future.

FORTUNE TELLER:

Keck!

SABINA:

All right, I'll tell *you* my future.

Laughing dreamily and tracing it out with one finger on the palm of her hand.

I've won the Beauty Contest in Atlantic City—well, I'll

win the Beauty Contest of the whole world. I'll take President Antrobus away from that wife of his. Then I'll take every man away from his wife. I'll turn the whole earth upside down.

FORTUNE TELLER:

Keck!

SABINA:

When all those husbands just think about me they'll get dizzy. They'll faint in the streets. They'll have to lean against lampposts. —Esmeralda, who was Helen of Troy?

FORTUNE TELLER:

Furiously.

Shut your foolish mouth. When Mr. Antrobus comes along you can see what you can do. Until then, —go away.

SABINA *laughs. As she returns to the door of her Bingo Parlor a group of* CONVEENERS *rush over and smother her with attentions: "Oh, Miss Lily, you know me. You've known me for years."*

SABINA:

Go away, boys, go away. I'm after bigger fry than you are. —Why, Mr. Simpson!! How *dare* you!! I expect that even you nobodies must have girls to amuse you; but where you find them and what you do with them is of absolutely no interest to me.

Exit. The CONVEENERS *squeal with pleasure and stumble in after her.*
The FORTUNE TELLER *rises, puts her pipe down on the stool, unfurls her voluminous skirts, gives a sharp wrench to her bodice and strolls towards the audience, swinging her hips like a young woman.*

FORTUNE TELLER:

I tell the future. Keck. Nothing easier. Everybody's future is in their face. Nothing easier.
But who can tell your past, —eh? Nobody!
Your youth, —where did it go? It slipped away while you weren't looking. While you were asleep. While you were drunk? Puh! You're like our friends, Mr. and Mrs. Antrobus; you lie awake nights trying to know your past. What did it mean? What was it trying to say to you?
Think! Think! Split your heads. I can't tell the past and neither can you. If anybody tries to tell you the past, take my word for it, they're charlatans! Charlatans! But I can tell the future.
She suddenly barks at a passing CHAIR PUSHER.
Apoplexy!
She returns to the audience.
Nobody listens. —Keck! I see a face among you now—I won't embarrass him by pointing him out, but, listen, it may be you: Next year the watchsprings inside you will crumple up. Death by regret, —Type Y. It's in the corners of your mouth. You'll decide that you should have lived for pleasure, but that you missed it. Death by regret, —Type Y. . . . Avoid mirrors. You'll try to be angry, —but no! —no anger.

Far forward, confidentially.

And now what's the immediate future of our friends, the Antrobuses? Oh, you've seen it as well as I have, keck, —that dizziness of the head; that Great Man dizziness? The inventor of beer and gunpowder. The sudden fits of temper and then the long stretches of inertia? "I'm a sultan; let my slave girls fan me"?

You know as well as I what's coming. Rain. Rain. Rain in floods. The deluge. But first you'll see shameful things—shameful things. Some of you will be saying: "Let him drown. He's not worth saving. Give the whole thing up." I can see it in your faces. But you're wrong. Keep your doubts and despairs to yourselves.

Again there'll be the narrow escape. The survival of a handful. From destruction, —total destruction.

She points sweeping with her hand to the stage.

Even of the animals, a few will be saved: two of a kind, male and female, two of a kind.

The heads of CONVEENERS *appear about the stage and in the orchestra pit, jeering at her.*

CONVEENERS:

Charlatan! Madam Killjoy! Mrs. Jeremiah! Charlatan!

FORTUNE TELLER:

And *you!* Mark my words before it's too late. Where'll *you* be?

CONVEENERS:

The croaking raven. Old dust and ashes. Rags, bottles, sacks.

FORTUNE TELLER:

Yes, stick out your tongues. You can't stick your tongues out far enough to lick the death sweat from your foreheads. It's too late to work now—bail out the flood with your soup spoons. You've had your chance and you've lost.

CONVEENERS:

Enjoy yourselves!!!

They disappear. The FORTUNE TELLER *looks off left and puts her finger on her lip.*

FORTUNE TELLER:

They're coming—the Antrobuses. Keck. Your hope. Your despair. Your selves.

Enter from the left, MR. *and* MRS. ANTROBUS *and* GLADYS.

MRS. ANTROBUS:

Gladys Antrobus, stick your stummick in.

GLADYS:

But it's easier this way.

MRS. ANTROBUS:

Well, it's too bad the new president has such a clumsy daughter, that's all I can say. Try and be a lady.

FORTUNE TELLER:

Aijah! That's been said a hundred billion times.

MRS. ANTROBUS:

Goodness! Where's Henry? He was here just a minute ago.
Henry!

Sudden violent stir. A roller chair appears from the left. About it are dancing in great excitement HENRY *and a Negro* CHAIR PUSHER.

HENRY:

Slingshot in hand.

I'll put your eye out. I'll make you yell, like you never yelled before.

CHAIR PUSHER:

At the same time.

Now, I warns you. I warns you. If you make me mad, you'll get hurt.

MR. ANTROBUS:

Henry! What is this? Put down that slingshot.

MRS. ANTROBUS:

At the same time.

Henry! HENRY! Behave yourself.

FORTUNE TELLER:

That's right, young man. There are too many people in the world as it is. Everybody's in the way, except one's self.

HENRY:

All I wanted to do was—have some fun.

CHAIR PUSHER:

Nobody can't touch my chair, nobody, without I allow 'em to. You get clean away from me and you get away fast.

He pushes his chair off, muttering.

MR. ANTROBUS:

What were you doing, Henry?

HENRY:

Everybody's always getting mad. Everybody's always trying to push you around. I'll make him sorry for this; I'll make him sorry.

MR. ANTROBUS:

Give me that slingshot.

HENRY:

I won't. I'm sorry I came to this place. I wish I weren't here. I wish I weren't anywhere.

MRS. ANTROBUS:

Now, Henry, don't get so excited about nothing. I declare I don't know what we're going to do with you. Put your slingshot in your pocket, and don't try to take hold of things that don't belong to you.

MR. ANTROBUS:

After this you can stay home. I wash my hands of you.

MRS. ANTROBUS:

Come now, let's forget all about it. Everybody take a good breath of that sea air and calm down.

A passing CONVEENER *bows to* MR. ANTROBUS *who nods to him.*

Who was that you spoke to, George?

MR. ANTROBUS:

Nobody, Maggie. Just the candidate who ran against me in the election.

MRS. ANTROBUS:

The man who ran against you in the election!!

She turns and waves her umbrella after the disappearing CONVEENER.

My husband didn't speak to you and he never will speak to you.

MR. ANTROBUS:

Now, Maggie.

MRS. ANTROBUS:

After those lies you told about him in your speeches! Lies, that's what they were.

GLADYS *and* HENRY:

Mama, everybody's looking at you. Everybody's laughing at you.

MRS. ANTROBUS:

If you must know, my husband's a SAINT, a downright SAINT, and you're not fit to speak to him on the street.

MR. ANTROBUS:

Now, Maggie, now, Maggie, that's enough of that.

MRS. ANTROBUS:

George Antrobus, you're a perfect worm. If you won't stand up for yourself, I will.

GLADYS:

Mama, you just act awful in public.

MRS. ANTROBUS:

Laughing.

Well, I must say I enjoyed it. I feel better. Wish his wife had been there to hear it. Children, what do you want to do?

GLADYS:

Papa, can we ride in one of those chairs? Mama, I want to ride in one of those chairs.

MRS. ANTROBUS:

No, sir. If you're tired you just sit where you are. We have no money to spend on foolishness.

MR. ANTROBUS:

I guess we have money enough for a thing like that. It's one of the things you do at Atlantic City.

MRS. ANTROBUS:

Oh, we have? I tell you it's a miracle my children have shoes to stand up in. I didn't think I'd ever live to see them pushed around in chairs.

MR. ANTROBUS:

We're on a vacation, aren't we? We have a right to some treats, I guess. Maggie, some day you're going to drive me crazy.

MRS. ANTROBUS:

All right, go. I'll just sit here and laugh at you. And you can give me my dollar right in my hand. Mark my words, a rainy day is coming. There's a rainy day ahead of us. I feel it in my bones. Go on, throw your money around. I can starve. I've starved before. I know how.

A CONVEENER *puts his head through Turkish Bath window and speaks, with raised eyebrows.*

CONVEENER:

Hello, George. How are ya? I see where you brought the WHOLE family along.

MRS. ANTROBUS:

And what do you mean by that?

CONVEENER *withdraws head and closes window.*

MR. ANTROBUS:

Maggie, I tell you there's a limit to what I can stand. God's

Heaven, haven't I worked *enough*? Don't I get *any* vacation? Can't I even give my children so much as a ride in a roller chair?

MRS. ANTROBUS:

Putting out her hand for raindrops.

Anyway, it's going to rain very soon and you have your broadcast to make.

MR. ANTROBUS:

Now, Maggie, I warn you. A man can stand a family only just so long. I'm warning you.

Enter SABINA *from the Bingo Parlor. She wears a flounced red silk bathing suit, 1905. Red stockings, shoes, parasol. She bows demurely to* MR. ANTROBUS *and starts down the ramp.* MR. ANTROBUS *and the children stare at her.* MR. ANTROBUS *bows gallantly.*

MRS. ANTROBUS:

Why, George Antrobus, how can you say such a thing! You have the best family in the world.

MR. ANTROBUS:

Good morning, Miss Fairweather.

SABINA *finally disappears behind the beach umbrella or in a cabana in the orchestra pit.*

MRS. ANTROBUS:

Who on earth was that you spoke to, George?

MR. ANTROBUS:

Complacent; mock-modest.

Hm . . . m . . . just a . . . solambaka keray.

MRS. ANTROBUS:

What? I can't understand you.

GLADYS:

Mama, wasn't she beautiful?

HENRY:

Papa, introduce her to me.

MRS. ANTROBUS:

Children, will you be quiet while I ask your father a simple question? —Who did you say it was, George?

MR. ANTROBUS:

Why-uh . . . a friend of mine. Very nice refined girl.

MRS. ANTROBUS:

I'm waiting.

MR. ANTROBUS:

Maggie, that's the girl I gave the prize to in the Beauty Contest—that's Miss Atlantic City 1942.

MRS. ANTROBUS:

Hm! She looked like Sabina to me.

HENRY:

At the railing.

Mama, the lifeguard knows her, too. Mama, he knows her well.

MR. ANTROBUS:

Henry, come here. —She's a very nice girl in every way and the sole support of her aged mother.

MRS. ANTROBUS:

So was Sabina, so was Sabina; and it took a wall of ice to open your eyes about Sabina. —Henry, come over and sit down on this bench.

MR. ANTROBUS:

She's a very different matter from Sabina. Miss Fairweather is a college graduate, Phi Beta Kappa.

MRS. ANTROBUS:

Henry, you sit here by Mama. Gladys—

MR. ANTROBUS:

Sitting.

Reduced circumstances have required her taking a position as hostess in a Bingo Parlor; but there isn't a girl with higher principles in the country.

MRS. ANTROBUS:

Well, let's not talk about it. —Henry, I haven't seen a whale yet.

MR. ANTROBUS:

She speaks seven languages and has more culture in her little finger than you've acquired in a lifetime.

MRS. ANTROBUS:

Assumed amiability.

All right, all right, George. I'm glad to know there are such superior girls in the Bingo Parlors. —Henry, what's that?

Pointing at the storm signal, which has one black disk.

HENRY:

What is it, Papa?

MR. ANTROBUS:

What? Oh, that's the storm signal. One of those black disks means bad weather; two means storm; three means hurricane; and four means the end of the world.

As they watch it, a second black disk rolls into place.

MRS. ANTROBUS:

Goodness! I'm going this very minute to buy you all some raincoats.

GLADYS:

Putting her cheek against her father's shoulder.

Mama, don't go yet. I like sitting this way. And the ocean coming in and coming in. Papa, don't you like it?

MRS. ANTROBUS:

Well, there's only one thing I lack to make me a perfectly happy woman: I'd like to see a whale.

HENRY:

Mama, we saw two. Right out there. They're delegates to the convention. I'll find you one.

GLADYS:

Papa, ask me something. Ask me a question.

MR. ANTROBUS:

Well . . . how big's the ocean?

GLADYS:

Papa, you're teasing me. It's—three hundred and sixty million square miles—and—it—covers—three-fourths—of—the—earth's—surface—and—its—deepest place—is—five—and—a—half— miles—deep—and—its—average—depth—is—twelve thousand—feet. No, Papa, ask me something hard, real hard.

MRS. ANTROBUS:

Rising.

Now I'm going off to buy those raincoats. I think that bad weather's going to get worse and worse. I hope it doesn't come before your broadcast. I should think we have about an hour or so.

HENRY:

I hope it comes and *zzzzzz* everything before it. I hope it—

MRS. ANTROBUS:

Henry! —George, I think . . . maybe, it's one of those storms that are just as bad on land as on the sea. When you're just as safe and safer in a good stout boat.

HENRY:

There's a boat out at the end of the pier.

MRS. ANTROBUS:

Well, keep your eye on it. George, you shut your eyes and get a good rest before the broadcast.

MR. ANTROBUS:

Thundering Judas, do I have to be told when to open and shut my eyes? Go and buy your raincoats.

MRS. ANTROBUS:

Now, children, you have ten minutes to walk around. Ten minutes. And, Henry: control yourself. Gladys, stick by your brother and don't get lost.

They run off.

Will you be all right, George?

CONVEENERS *suddenly stick their heads out of the Bingo Parlor and Salt Water Taffy store, and voices rise from the orchestra pit.*

CONVEENERS:

George, Geo-r-r-rge! George! Leave the old hen coop at home, George. Do-mes-ticated Georgie!

MRS. ANTROBUS:

Shaking her umbrella.

Low common oafs! That's what they are. Guess a man has a right to bring his wife to a convention, if he wants to.

She starts off.

What's the matter with a family, I'd like to know. What else have they got to offer?

Exit. MR. ANTROBUS *has closed his eyes. The* FORTUNE TELLER *comes out of her shop and goes over to the left proscenium. She leans against it watching* SABINA *quizzically.*

FORTUNE TELLER:

Heh! Here she comes!

SABINA:

Loud whisper.

What's he doing?

FORTUNE TELLER:

Oh, he's ready for you. Bite your lips, dear, take a long breath and come on up.

SABINA:

I'm nervous. My whole future depends on this. I'm nervous.

FORTUNE TELLER:

Don't be a fool. What more could you want? He's forty-five. His head's a little dizzy. He's just been elected president. He's never known any other woman than his wife. Whenever he looks at her he realizes that she knows every foolish thing he's ever done.

SABINA:

Still whispering.

I don't know why it is, but every time I start one of these I'm nervous.

FORTUNE TELLER:

You make me tired.

SABINA:

First tell me my future.

The FORTUNE TELLER *laughs drily and makes the gesture of brushing away a nonsensical question. She stands in the center of the stage watching the following scene.*

SABINA *coughs and speaks.*

Oh, Mr. Antrobus, —dare I speak to you for a moment?

MR. ANTROBUS:

What? —Oh, certainly, certainly, Miss Fairweather.

SABINA:

Mr. Antrobus . . . I've been so unhappy. I've wanted . . . I've wanted to make sure that you don't think that I'm the kind of girl who goes out for beauty contests.

FORTUNE TELLER:

That's the way!

MR. ANTROBUS:

Oh, I understand. I understand perfectly.

FORTUNE TELLER:

Give it a little more. Lean on it.

SABINA:

I knew you would. My mother said to me this morning: Lily, she said, that fine Mr. Antrobus gave you the prize because he saw at once that you weren't the kind of girl who'd go in for a thing like that. But, honestly, Mr. Antrobus, in this world, honestly, a good girl doesn't know where to turn.

FORTUNE TELLER:

Now you've gone too far.

MR. ANTROBUS:

My dear Miss Fairweather!

SABINA:

You wouldn't know how hard it is. With that lovely wife and daughter you have. Oh, I think Mrs. Antrobus is the finest woman I ever saw. I wish I were like her.

MR. ANTROBUS:

There, there. There's . . . uh . . . room for all kinds of people in the world, Miss Fairweather.

SABINA:

How wonderful of you to say that. How generous! —Mr. Antrobus, have you a moment free? . . . I'm afraid I may be a little conspicuous here. . . . Could you come down, for just a moment, to my beach cabana . . . ?

MR. ANTROBUS:

Why-uh . . . yes, certainly . . . for a moment . . . just for a moment.

SABINA:

There's a deck chair there. Because: you know you *do* look tired. Just this morning my mother said to me: Lily, she said, I hope Mr. Antrobus is getting a good rest. His fine strong face has deep deep lines in it. Now isn't it true, Mr. Antrobus: you work too hard?

FORTUNE TELLER:

Bingo!

She goes into her shop.

SABINA:

Now you will just stretch out. No, I shan't say a word, not a word. I shall just sit there, —privileged. That's what I am.

MR. ANTROBUS:

Taking her hand.

Miss Fairweather . . . you'll . . . spoil me.

SABINA:

Just a moment. I have something I wish to say to the audience.
—Ladies and gentlemen. I'm not going to play this particular scene tonight. It's just a short scene and we're going to skip it. But I'll tell you what takes place and then we can continue the play from there on. Now in this scene—

MR. ANTROBUS:

Between his teeth.
But, Miss Somerset!

SABINA:

I'm sorry. I'm sorry. But I have to skip it. In this scene, I talk to Mr. Antrobus, and at the end of it he decides to leave his wife, get a divorce at Reno, and marry me. That's all.

MR. ANTROBUS:

Fitz! —Fitz!

SABINA:

So that now I've told you we can jump to the end of it, —where you say:
Enter in fury MR. FITZPATRICK, *the* STAGE MANAGER.

MR. FITZPATRICK:

Miss Somerset, we insist on your playing this scene.

SABINA:

I'm sorry, Mr. Fitzpatrick, but I can't and I won't. I've told the audience all they need to know and now we can go on.

Other actors begin to appear on the stage, listening.

MR. FITZPATRICK:

And *why* can't you play it?

SABINA:

Because there are some lines in that scene that would hurt some people's feelings and I don't think the theatre is a place where people's feelings ought to be hurt.

MR. FITZPATRICK:

Miss Somerset, you can pack up your things and go home. I shall call the understudy and I shall report you to Equity.

SABINA:

I sent the understudy up to the corner for a cup of coffee and if Equity tries to penalize me I'll drag the case right up to the Supreme Court. Now listen, everybody, there's no need to get excited.

MR. FITZPATRICK *and* MR. ANTROBUS:

Why can't you play it? . . . What's the matter with the scene?

SABINA:

Well, if you must know, I have a personal guest in the audience tonight. Her life hasn't been exactly a happy one. I wouldn't have my friend hear some of these lines for the whole world. I don't suppose it occurred to the author that some other women might have gone through the experience of losing their husbands like this. Wild horses wouldn't drag from me the details of my friend's life, but . . . well, they'd been married twenty years, and before he got rich, why, she'd done the washing and everything.

MR. FITZPATRICK:

Miss Somerset, your friend will forgive you. We must play this scene.

SABINA:

Nothing, nothing will make me say some of those lines . . . about "a man outgrows a wife every seven years" and . . . and that one about "the Mohammedans being the only people who looked the subject square in the face." Nothing.

MR. FITZPATRICK:

Miss Somerset! Go to your dressing room. I'll *read* your lines.

SABINA:

Now everybody's nerves are on edge.

MR. ANTROBUS:

Skip the scene.

MR. FITZPATRICK *and the other actors go off.*

SABINA:

Thank you. I knew you'd understand. We'll do just what I said. So Mr. Antrobus is going to divorce his wife and marry me. Mr. Antrobus, you say: "It won't be easy to lay all this before my wife."

MR. ANTROBUS:

Walks about, his hand to his forehead, muttering.

Wait a minute. I can't get back into it as easily as all that. "My wife is a very obstinate woman." Hm . . . then you say . . . hm . . . Miss Fairweather, I mean Lily, it won't be easy to lay all this before my wife. It'll hurt her feelings a little.

SABINA:

Listen, George: *other* people haven't got feelings. Not in the same way that we have, —we who are presidents like you and prize winners like me. Listen, other people haven't got feelings; they just imagine they have. Within two weeks they go back to playing bridge and going to the movies.

Listen, dear: everybody in the world except a few people like you and me are just people of straw. Most people have no insides at all. Now that you're president you'll see that. Listen, darling, there's a kind of secret society at the top of the world, —like you and me, —that know this. The

world was made for us. What's life anyway? Except for two things, pleasure and power, what is life? Boredom! Foolishness. You know it is. Except for those two things, life's nau-se-at-ing.
So, —come here!

She moves close. They kiss.

So.
Now when your wife comes, it's really very simple; just tell her.

MR. ANTROBUS:

Lily, Lily: you're a wonderful woman.

SABINA:

Of course I am.

They enter the cabana and it hides them from view. Distant roll of thunder. A third black disk appears on the weather signal. Distant thunder is heard. MRS. ANTROBUS *appears carrying parcels. She looks about, seats herself on the bench left, and fans herself with her handkerchief. Enter* GLADYS *right, followed by two* CONVEENERS. *She is wearing red stockings.*

MRS. ANTROBUS:

Gladys!

GLADYS:

Mama, here I am.

MRS. ANTROBUS:

Gladys Antrobus!!! Where did you get those dreadful things?

GLADYS:

Wha-a-t? Papa liked the color.

MRS. ANTROBUS:

You go back to the hotel this minute!

GLADYS:

I won't. I won't. Papa liked the color.

MRS. ANTROBUS:

All right. All right. You stay here. I've a good mind to let your father see you that way. You stay right here.

GLADYS:

I . . . I don't want to stay if . . . if you don't think he'd like it.

MRS. ANTROBUS:

Oh . . . it's all one to me. I don't care what happens. I don't care if the biggest storm in the whole world comes. Let it come.

She folds her hands.

Where's your brother?

GLADYS:

In a small voice.

He'll be here.

MRS. ANTROBUS:

Will he? Well, let him get into trouble. I don't care. I don't know where your father is, I'm sure.

Laughter from the cabana.

GLADYS:

Leaning over the rail.

I think he's . . . Mama, he's talking to the lady in the red dress.

MRS. ANTROBUS:

Is that so?

Pause.

We'll wait till he's through. Sit down here beside me and stop fidgeting. . . . What are you crying about?

Distant thunder. She covers Gladys' stockings with a raincoat.

GLADYS:

You don't like my stockings.

Two CONVEENERS *rush in with a microphone on a standard and various paraphernalia. The* FORTUNE TELLER *appears at the door of her shop. Other characters gradually gather.*

BROADCAST OFFICIAL:

Mrs. Antrobus! Thank God we've found you at last. Where's Mr. Antrobus? We've been hunting everywhere for him. It's about time for the broadcast to the conventions of the world.

MRS. ANTROBUS:

Calm.

I expect he'll be here in a minute.

BROADCAST OFFICIAL:

Mrs. Antrobus, if he doesn't show up in time, I hope you will consent to broadcast in his place. It's the most important broadcast of the year.

SABINA *enters from cabana, followed by* MR. ANTROBUS.

MRS. ANTROBUS:

No, I shan't. I haven't one single thing to say.

BROADCAST OFFICIAL:

Then won't you help us find him, Mrs. Antrobus? A storm's coming up. A hurricane. A deluge!

SECOND CONVEENER:

Who has sighted MR. ANTROBUS *over the rail.*

Joe! Joe! Here he is.

BROADCAST OFFICIAL:

In the name of God, Mr. Antrobus, you're on the air in five minutes. Will you kindly please come and test the instrument? That's all we ask. If you just please begin the alphabet slowly.

MR. ANTROBUS, *with set face, comes ponderously up the ramp. He stops at the point where his waist is level with the stage and speaks authoritatively to the* OFFICIALS.

MR. ANTROBUS:

I'll be ready when the time comes. Until then, move away. Go away. I have something I wish to say to my wife.

BROADCAST OFFICIAL:

Whimpering.

Mr. Antrobus! This is the most important broadcast of the year.

The OFFICIALS *withdraw to the edge of the stage.*

SABINA *glides up the ramp behind* MR. ANTROBUS.

SABINA:

Whispering.

Don't let her argue. Remember arguments have nothing to do with it.

MR. ANTROBUS:

Maggie, I'm moving out of the hotel. In fact, I'm moving out of everything. For good. I'm going to marry Miss Fairweather. I shall provide generously for you and the children. In a few years you'll be able to see that it's all for the best.

That's all I have to say.

BROADCAST OFFICIAL:	BINGO CALLER:
Mr. Antrobus! I hope you'll be ready. This is the most important broadcast of the year.	A-nine; A-nine. D-forty-two; D-forty-two. C-thirty; C-thirty. B-seventeen; B-seventeen. C-forty; C-forty.

GLADYS:

What did Papa say, Mama? I didn't hear what Papa said.

CHORUS:

Bingo!!

BROADCAST OFFICIAL:

Mr. Antrobus. All we want to do is test your voice with the alphabet.

MR. ANTROBUS:

Go away. Clear out.

MRS. ANTROBUS:

Composedly with lowered eyes.

George, I can't talk to you until you wipe those silly red marks off your face.

MR. ANTROBUS:

I think there's nothing to talk about. I've said what I have to say.

SABINA:

Splendid!!

MR. ANTROBUS:

You're a fine woman, Maggie, but . . . but a man has his own life to lead in the world.

MRS. ANTROBUS:

Well, after living with you for five thousand years I guess I have a right to a word or two, haven't I?

MR. ANTROBUS:

To SABINA.

What can I answer to that?

SABINA:

Tell her that conversation would only hurt her feelings. It's-kinder-in-the-long-run-to-do-it-short-and-quick.

MR. ANTROBUS:

I want to spare your feelings in every way I can, Maggie.

BROADCAST OFFICIAL:

Mr. Antrobus, the hurricane signal's gone up. We could begin right now.

MRS. ANTROBUS:

Calmly, almost dreamily.

I didn't marry you because you were perfect. I didn't even marry you because I loved you. I married you because you gave me a promise.

She takes off her ring and looks at it.

That promise made up for your faults. And the promise I gave you made up for mine. Two imperfect people got married and it was the promise that made the marriage.

MR. ANTROBUS:

Maggie, . . . I was only nineteen.

MRS. ANTROBUS:

She puts her ring back on her finger.

And when our children were growing up, it wasn't a house that protected them; and it wasn't our love that protected them—it was that promise.

And when that promise is broken—this can happen!

With a sweep of the hand she removes the raincoat from Gladys' stockings.

MR. ANTROBUS:

Stretches out his arm, apoplectic.

Gladys!! Have you gone crazy? Has everyone gone crazy?

Turning on SABINA.

You did this. You gave them to her.

SABINA:

I never said a word to her.

MR. ANTROBUS:

To GLADYS.

You go back to the hotel and take those horrible things off.

GLADYS:

Pert.

Before I go, I've got something to tell you— It's about Henry.

MRS. ANTROBUS:

Claps her hands peremptorily.

Stop your noise— I'm taking her back to the hotel, George.

Before I go I have a letter. . . . I have a message to throw into the ocean.

Fumbling in her handbag.

Where is the plagued thing? Here it is.

She flings something—invisible to us—far over the heads of the audience to the back of the auditorium.

It's a bottle. And in the bottle's a letter. And in the letter is written all the things that a woman knows.

It's never been told to any man and it's never been told to any woman, and if it finds its destination, a new time will come. We're not what books and plays say we are. We're not what advertisements say we are. We're not in the movies and we're not on the radio.

We're not what you're all told and what you think we are: We're ourselves. And if any man can find one of us he'll learn why the whole universe was set in motion. And if any man harm any one of us, his soul—the only soul he's got—had better be at the bottom of that ocean, —and that's the only way to put it. Gladys, come here. We're going back to the hotel.

She drags GLADYS *firmly off by the hand, but* GLADYS *breaks away and comes down to speak to her father.*

SABINA:

Such goings on. Don't give it a minute's thought.

GLADYS:

Anyway, I think you ought to know that Henry hit a man with a stone. He hit one of those colored men that push the chairs and the man's very sick. Henry ran away and hid and some policemen are looking for him very hard.

And I don't care a bit if you don't want to have anything to do with Mama and me, because I'll never like you again and I hope nobody ever likes you again, —so there!

She runs off. MR. ANTROBUS *starts after her.*

MR. ANTROBUS:

I . . . I have to go and see what I can do about this.

SABINA:

You stay right here. Don't you go now while you're excited. Gracious sakes, all these things will be forgotten in a hundred years. Come, now, you're on the air. Just say anything—it doesn't matter what. Just a lot of birds and fishes and things.

BROADCAST OFFICIAL:

Thank you, Miss Fairweather. Thank you very much. Ready, Mr. Antrobus.

MR. ANTROBUS:

Touching the microphone.

What is it, what is it? Who am I talking to?

BROADCAST OFFICIAL:

Why, Mr. Antrobus! To our Order and to all the other Orders.

MR. ANTROBUS:

Raising his head.

What are all those birds doing?

BROADCAST OFFICIAL:

Those are just a few of the birds. Those are the delegates to our convention, —two of a kind.

MR. ANTROBUS:

Pointing into the audience.

Look at the water. Look at them all. Those fishes jumping. The children should see this! —There's Maggie's whales!! Here are your whales, Maggie!!

BROADCAST OFFICIAL:

I hope you're ready, Mr. Antrobus.

MR. ANTROBUS:

And look on the beach! You didn't tell me these would be here!

SABINA:

Yes, George. Those are the animals.

BROADCAST OFFICIAL:

Busy with the apparatus.

Yes, Mr. Antrobus, those are the vertebrates. We hope the lion will have a word to say when you're through. Step right up, Mr. Antrobus, we're ready. We'll just have time before the storm.

Pause. In a hoarse whisper.

They're wait-ing.

It has grown dark. Soon after he speaks, a high whistling noise begins. Strange veering lights start whirling about the stage. The other characters disappear from the stage.

MR. ANTROBUS:

Friends. Cousins. Four score and ten billion years ago our forefather brought forth upon this planet the spark of life—

He is drowned out by thunder. When the thunder stops, the FORTUNE TELLER *is seen standing beside him.*

FORTUNE TELLER:

Antrobus, there's not a minute to be lost. Don't you see the four disks on the weather signal? Take your family into that boat at the end of the pier.

MR. ANTROBUS:

My family? I have no family. Maggie! Maggie! —They won't come.

FORTUNE TELLER:

They'll come. —Antrobus! Take these animals into that boat with you. All of them, —two of each kind.

SABINA:

George, what's the matter with you? This is just a storm like any other storm.

MR. ANTROBUS:

Maggie!

SABINA:

Stay with me, we'll go . . .

Losing conviction.

This is just another thunderstorm, —isn't it? Isn't it?

MR. ANTROBUS:

Maggie!!!

MRS. ANTROBUS *appears beside him with* GLADYS.

MRS. ANTROBUS:

Matter-of-fact.

Here I am and here's Gladys.

MR. ANTROBUS:

Where've you been? Where have you been? Quick, we're going into that boat out there.

MRS. ANTROBUS:

I know we are. But I haven't found Henry.

She wanders off into the darkness calling "Henry!"

SABINA:

Low urgent babbling, only occasionally raising her voice.

I don't believe it. I don't believe it's anything at all. I've seen hundreds of storms like this.

FORTUNE TELLER:

There's no time to lose. Go. Push the animals along before you. Start a new world. Begin again.

SABINA:

Esmeralda! George! Tell me, —is it really serious?

MR. ANTROBUS:

Suddenly very busy.

Elephants first. Gently, gently. —Look where you're going.

GLADYS:

Leaning over the ramp and striking an animal on the back.
Stop it or you'll be left behind!

MR. ANTROBUS:

Is the kangaroo there? *There* you are! Take those turtles in your pouch, will you?
To some other animals, pointing to his shoulder.
Here! You jump up here. You'll be trampled on.

GLADYS:

To her father, pointing below.
Papa, look, —the snakes!

MRS. ANTROBUS:

I can't find Henry. Hen-ry!

MR. ANTROBUS:

Go along. Go along. Climb on their backs. —Wolves! Jackals, —whatever you are, —tend to your own business!

GLADYS:

Pointing, tenderly.
Papa, —look.

SABINA:

Mr. Antrobus—take me with you. Don't leave me here. I'll work. I'll help. I'll do anything.

Three CONVEENERS *cross the stage, marching with a banner.*

CONVEENERS:

George! What are you scared of? —George! Fellas, it looks like rain. —"Maggie, where's my umbrella?" —George, setting up for Barnum and Bailey.

MR. ANTROBUS:

Again catching his wife's hand.

Come on now, Maggie, —the pier's going to break any minute.

MRS. ANTROBUS:

I'm not going a step without Henry. Henry!

GLADYS:

On the ramp.

Mama! Papa! Hurry. The pier's cracking, Mama. It's going to break.

MRS. ANTROBUS:

Henry! Cain! CAIN!

HENRY *dashes onto the stage and joins his mother.*

HENRY:

Here I am, Mama.

MRS. ANTROBUS:

Thank God! —Now come quick.

HENRY:

I didn't think you wanted me.

MRS. ANTROBUS:

Quick!

She pushes him down before her into the aisle.

All the ANTROBUSES *are now in the theatre aisle.*

SABINA *stands at the top of the ramp.*

SABINA:

Mrs. Antrobus, take me. Don't you remember me? I'll work. I'll help. Don't leave me here!

MRS. ANTROBUS:

Impatiently, but as though it were of no importance.

Yes, yes. There's a lot of work to be done. Only hurry.

FORTUNE TELLER:

Now dominating the stage. To SABINA *with a grim smile.*

Yes, go—back to the kitchen with you.

SABINA:

Half down the ramp. To FORTUNE TELLER.

I don't know why my life's always being interrupted—just when everything's going fine!!

She dashes up the aisle.

Now the CONVEENERS *emerge doing a serpentine dance on the stage. They jeer at the* FORTUNE TELLER.

CONVEENERS:

Get a canoe—there's not a minute to be lost! Tell me my future, Mrs. Croaker.

FORTUNE TELLER:

Paddle in the water, boys—enjoy yourselves.

BINGO CALLER:

A-nine; A-nine. C-twenty-four. C-twenty-four.

CONVEENERS:

Rags, bottles, and sacks.

FORTUNE TELLER:

Go back and climb on your roofs. Put rags in the cracks under your doors. —Nothing will keep out the flood. You've had your chance. You've had your day. You've failed. You've lost.

BINGO CALLER:

B-fifteen. B-fifteen.

FORTUNE TELLER:

Shading her eyes and looking out to sea.

They're safe. George Antrobus! Think it over! A new world to make. —Think it over!

CURTAIN

Act Three

·⁘·⁘·⁘·⁘·⁘·

Just before the curtain rises, two sounds are heard from the stage: a cracked bugle call.

The curtain rises on almost total darkness. Almost all the flats composing the walls of Mr. Antrobus' house, as of Act I, are up, but they lean helter-skelter against one another, leaving irregular gaps. Among the flats missing are two in the back wall, leaving the frames of the window and door crazily out of line. Offstage, back right, some red Roman fire is burning. The bugle call is repeated. Enter SABINA *through the tilted door. She is dressed as a Napoleonic camp follower, "la fille du régiment," in begrimed reds and blues.*

SABINA:

Mrs. Antrobus! Gladys! Where are you?

The war's over. The war's over. You can come out. The peace treaty's been signed.

Where are they? —Hmpf! Are they dead, too? Mrs. Annnntrobus! Glaaaadus! Mr. Antrobus'll be here this afternoon. I just saw him downtown. Huuuurry and put things in order. He says that now that the war's over we'll all have to settle down and be perfect.

Enter MR. FITZPATRICK, *the* STAGE MANAGER, *followed by the whole company, who stand waiting at the edges of the stage.* MR. FITZPATRICK *tries to interrupt* SABINA.

MR. FITZPATRICK:

Miss Somerset, we have to stop a moment.

SABINA:

They may be hiding out in the back—

MR. FITZPATRICK:

Miss Somerset! We have to stop a moment.

SABINA:

What's the matter?

MR. FITZPATRICK:

There's an explanation we have to make to the audience. —Lights, please.

To the actor who plays MR. ANTROBUS.

Will you explain the matter to the audience?

The lights go up. We now see that a balcony or elevated runway has been erected at the back of the stage, back of the wall of the Antrobus house. From its extreme right and left ends, ladderlike steps descend to the floor of the stage.

MR. ANTROBUS:

Ladies and gentlemen, an unfortunate accident has taken place backstage. Perhaps I should say *another* unfortunate accident.

SABINA:

I'm sorry. I'm sorry.

MR. ANTROBUS:

The management feels, in fact we all feel, that you are due an apology. And now we have to ask your indulgence for the most serious mishap of all. Seven of our actors have . . . have been taken ill. Apparently, it was something they ate. I'm not exactly clear what happened.

All the actors start to talk at once. MR. ANTROBUS *raises his hand.*

Now, now—not all at once. Fitz, do you know what it was?

MR. FITZPATRICK:

Why, it's perfectly clear. These seven actors had dinner together, and they ate something that disagreed with them.

SABINA:

Disagreed with them!!! They have ptomaine poisoning. They're in Bellevue Hospital this very minute in agony. They're having their stomachs pumped out this very minute, in perfect agony.

MR. ANTROBUS:

Fortunately, we've just heard they'll all recover.

SABINA:

It'll be a miracle if they do, a downright miracle. It was the lemon meringue pie.

ACTORS:

It was the fish . . . it was the canned tomatoes . . . it was the fish.

SABINA:

It was the lemon meringue pie. I saw it with my own eyes; it had blue mold all over the bottom of it.

MR. ANTROBUS:

Whatever it was, they're in no condition to take part in this performance. Naturally, we haven't enough understudies to fill all those roles; but we do have a number of splendid volunteers who have kindly consented to help us out. These friends have watched our rehearsals, and they assure me that they know the lines and the business very well. Let me introduce them to you—my dresser, Mr. Tremayne, —himself a distinguished Shakespearean actor for many years; our wardrobe mistress, Hester; Miss Somerset's maid, Ivy; and Fred Bailey, captain of the ushers in this theatre.

These persons bow modestly. IVY *and* HESTER *are colored girls.* Now this scene takes place near the end of the act. And I'm sorry to say we'll need a short rehearsal, just a short run-through. And as some of it takes place in the auditorium, we'll have to keep the curtain up. Those of you who wish can go out in the lobby and smoke some more. The rest of you can listen to us, or . . . or just talk quietly among yourselves, as you choose. Thank you. Now will you take it over, Mr. Fitzpatrick?

MR. FITZPATRICK:

Thank you. —Now for those of you who are listening, perhaps I should explain that at the end of this act, the men have come back from the war and the family's settled down in the house. And the author wants to show the hours of the night passing by over their heads, and the planets crossing the sky . . . uh . . . over their heads. And he says—this is hard to explain—that each of the hours of the night is a philosopher, or a great thinker. Eleven o'clock, for instance, is Aristotle. And nine o'clock is Spinoza. Like that. I don't suppose it means anything. It's just a kind of poetic effect.

SABINA:

Not mean anything! Why, it certainly does. Twelve o'clock goes by saying those wonderful things. I think it means that when people are asleep they have all those lovely thoughts, much better than when they're awake.

IVY:

Excuse me, I think it means— Excuse me, Mr. Fitzpatrick—

SABINA:

What were you going to say, Ivy?

IVY:

Mr. Fitzpatrick, you let my father come to a rehearsal; and my father's a Baptist minister, and he said that the author meant that—just like the hours and stars go by over our heads at night, in the same way the ideas and thoughts of the great men are in the air around us all the time and they're working on us, even when we don't know it.

MR. FITZPATRICK:

Well, well, maybe that's it. Thank you, Ivy. Anyway, —the hours of the night are philosophers. My friends, are you ready? Ivy, can you be eleven o'clock? "This good estate of the mind possessing its object in energy we call divine." Aristotle.

IVY:

Yes, sir. I know that and I know twelve o'clock and I know nine o'clock.

MR. FITZPATRICK:

Twelve o'clock? Mr. Tremayne, the Bible.

MR. TREMAYNE:

Yes.

MR. FITZPATRICK:

Ten o'clock? Hester, —Plato?

She nods eagerly.

Nine o'clock, Spinoza, —Fred?

FRED BAILEY:

Yes, *sir*.

FRED BAILEY *picks up a great gilded cardboard numeral IX and starts up the steps to the platform.*

MR. FITZPATRICK *strikes his forehead.*

MR. FITZPATRICK:

The planets!! We forgot all about the planets.

SABINA:

O my God! The planets! Are they sick too?

Actors nod.

MR. FITZPATRICK:

Ladies and gentlemen, the planets are singers. Of course, we can't replace them, so you'll have to imagine them singing in this scene. Saturn sings from the orchestra pit down here. The moon is way up there. And Mars with a red lantern in his hand, stands in the aisle over there— Tz-tz-tz. It's too bad; it all makes a very fine effect. However! Ready—nine o'clock: Spinoza.

FRED BAILEY:

Walking slowly across the balcony, left to right.

"After experience had taught me that the common occurrences of daily life are vain and futile—"

MR. FITZPATRICK:

Louder, Fred. "And I saw that all the objects of my desire and fear—"

FRED BAILEY:

"And I saw that all the objects of my desire and fear were in themselves nothing good nor bad save insofar as the mind was affected by them—"

MR. FITZPATRICK:

Do you know the rest? All right. Ten o'clock. Hester. Plato.

HESTER:

"Then tell me, O Critias, how will a man choose the ruler that shall rule over him? Will he not—"

MR. FITZPATRICK:

Thank you. Skip to the end, Hester.

HESTER:

". . . can be multiplied a thousand fold in its effects among the citizens."

MR. FITZPATRICK:

Thank you. —Aristotle, Ivy?

IVY:

"This good estate of the mind possessing its object in energy we call divine. This we mortals have occasionally and it is this energy which is pleasantest and best. But God has it always. It is wonderful in us; but in Him how much more wonderful."

MR. FITZPATRICK:

Midnight. Midnight, Mr. Tremayne. That's right, — you've done it before. —All right, everybody. You know what you have to do. —Lower the curtain. Houselights up. Act Three of THE SKIN OF OUR TEETH.

As the curtain descends.

You volunteers, just wear what you have on. Don't try to put on the costumes today.

Houselights go down. The act begins again. The Bugle call. Curtain rises. Enter SABINA.

SABINA:

Mrs. Antrobus! Gladys! Where are you?
The war's over. —You've heard all this—

She gabbles the main points.

Where—are—they? Are—they—dead, too, et cetera.
I—just—saw—Mr.—Antrobus—downtown, et cetera.

Slowing up.

He says that now that the war's over we'll all have to settle down and be perfect. They may be hiding out in the back somewhere. Mrs. An-tro-bus.

She wanders off. It has grown lighter.

A trapdoor is cautiously raised and MRS. ANTROBUS *emerges waist-high and listens. She is disheveled and worn; she wears a tattered dress and a shawl half covers her head. She talks down through the trapdoor.*

MRS. ANTROBUS:

It's getting light. There's still something burning over there—Newark, or Jersey City. What? Yes, I could swear I heard someone moving about up here. But I can't see anybody. I say: I can't see anybody.

She starts to move about the stage. Gladys' head appears at the trapdoor. She is holding a baby.

GLADYS:

Oh, Mama. Be careful.

MRS. ANTROBUS:

Now, Gladys, you stay out of sight.

GLADYS:

Well, let me stay here just a minute. I want the baby to get some of this fresh air.

MRS. ANTROBUS:

All right, but keep your eyes open. I'll see what I can find. I'll have a good hot plate of soup for you before you can say Jack Robinson. Gladys Antrobus! Do you know what I think I see? There's old Mr. Hawkins sweeping the sidewalk in front of his A&P store. Sweeping it with a broom. Why, he must have gone crazy, like the others! I see some other people moving about, too.

GLADYS:

Mama, come back, come back.

MRS. ANTROBUS *returns to the trapdoor and listens.*

MRS. ANTROBUS:

Gladys, there's something in the air. Everybody's movement's sort of different. I see some women walking right out in the middle of the street.

SABINA:

Offstage.

Mrs. An-tro-bus!

MRS. ANTROBUS *and* GLADYS:

What's that?!!

SABINA:

Offstage.

Glaaaadys! Mrs. An-tro-bus!

Enter SABINA.

MRS. ANTROBUS:

Gladys, that's Sabina's voice as sure as I live. —Sabina! Sabina! —Are you *alive?!!*

SABINA:

Of course, I'm alive. How've you girls been? *—Don't* try and kiss me. I never want to kiss another human being as long as I live. Sh-sh, there's nothing to get emotional about. Pull yourself together, the war's over. Take a deep breath, —the war's over.

MRS. ANTROBUS:

The war's over!! I don't believe you. I don't believe you. I can't believe you.

GLADYS:

Mama!

SABINA:

Who's that?

MRS. ANTROBUS:

That's Gladys and her baby. I don't believe you. Gladys, Sabina says the war's over. Oh, Sabina.

SABINA:

Leaning over the baby.

Goodness! Are there any babies left in the world! Can it *see*? And can it cry and everything?

GLADYS:

Yes, he can. He notices everything very well.

SABINA:

Where on earth did you get it? Oh, I won't ask. —Lord, I've lived all these seven years around camp and I've forgotten how to behave. —Now we've got to think about the men coming home. —Mrs. Antrobus, go and wash your face, I'm ashamed of you. Put your best clothes on. Mr. Antrobus'll be here this afternoon. I just saw him downtown.

MRS. ANTROBUS *and* GLADYS:

He's alive!! He'll be here!! Sabina, you're not joking?

MRS. ANTROBUS:

And Henry?

SABINA:

Dryly.

Yes, Henry's alive, too, that's what they say. Now don't stop to talk. Get yourselves fixed up. Gladys, you look terrible. Have you any decent clothes?

SABINA *has pushed them toward the trapdoor.*

MRS. ANTROBUS:

Half down.

Yes, I've something to wear just for this very day. But, Sabina, —who won the war?

SABINA:

Don't stop now—just wash your face.

A whistle sounds in the distance.

Oh, my God, what's that silly little noise?

MRS. ANTROBUS:

Why, it sounds like . . . it sounds like what used to be the noon whistle at the shoe-polish factory.

Exit.

SABINA:

That's what it is. Seems to me like peacetime's coming along pretty fast—shoe polish!

GLADYS:

Half down.

Sabina, how soon after peacetime begins does the milkman start coming to the door?

SABINA:

As soon as he catches a cow. Give him time to catch a cow, dear.

Exit GLADYS. SABINA *walks about a moment, thinking.*

Shoe polish! My, I'd forgotten what peacetime was like.

She shakes her head, then sits down by the trapdoor and starts talking down the hole.

Mrs. Antrobus, guess what I saw Mr. Antrobus doing this morning at dawn. He was tacking up a piece of paper on the door of the Town Hall. You'll die when you hear: it was a recipe for grass soup, for a grass soup that doesn't give you the diarrhea. Mr. Antrobus is still thinking up new things. —He told me to give you his love. He's got all sorts of ideas for peacetime, he says. No more laziness and idiocy, he says. And oh, yes! Where are his books? What? Well, pass them up. The first thing he wants to see are his books. He says if you've burnt those books, or if the rats have eaten them, he says it isn't worthwhile starting over again. Everybody's going to be beautiful, he says, and diligent, and very intelligent.

A hand reaches up with two volumes.

What language is that? Pu-u-gh, —mold! And he's got such plans for you, Mrs. Antrobus. You're going to study history and algebra—and so are Gladys and I—and philosophy. You should hear him talk.

Taking two more volumes.

Well, these are in English, anyway. —To hear him talk, seems like he expects you to be a combination, Mrs. Antrobus, of a saint and a college professor, and a dancehall hostess, if you know what I mean.

Two more volumes.

Ugh. German!

She is lying on the floor; one elbow bent, her cheek on her hand, meditatively.

Yes, peace will be here before we know it. In a week or two we'll be asking the Perkinses in for a quiet evening of bridge. We'll turn on the radio and hear how to be big successes with a new toothpaste. We'll trot down to the movies and see how girls with wax faces live—all *that* will begin again. Oh, Mrs. Antrobus, God forgive me but I enjoyed the war. Everybody's at their best in wartime. I'm sorry it's over.

And, oh, I forgot! Mr. Antrobus sent you another message—can you hear me?

Enter HENRY, *blackened and sullen. He is wearing torn overalls, but has one gaudy admiral's epaulette hanging by a thread from his right shoulder, and there are vestiges of gold and scarlet braid running down his left trouser leg. He stands listening.*

Listen! Henry's never to put foot in this house again, he says. He'll kill Henry on sight, if he sees him.

You don't know about Henry??? Well, where have you been? What? Well, Henry rose right to the top. Top of *what?* Listen, I'm telling you. Henry rose from corporal to captain, to major, to general. —I don't know how to say it, but the enemy is *Henry*; Henry *is* the enemy. Everybody knows that.

HENRY:

He'll kill me, will he?

SABINA:

Who are *you?* I'm not afraid of you. The war's over.

HENRY:

I'll kill him so fast. I've spent seven years trying to find him; the others I killed were just substitutes.

SABINA:

Goodness! It's Henry!

He makes an angry gesture.

Oh, I'm not afraid of you. The war's over, Henry Antrobus, and you're not any more important than any other unemployed. You go away and hide yourself, until we calm your father down.

HENRY:

The first thing to do is to burn up those old books; it's the ideas he gets out of those old books that . . . that makes the whole world so you can't live in it.

He reels forward and starts kicking the books about, but suddenly falls down in a sitting position.

SABINA:

You leave those books alone!! Mr. Antrobus is looking forward to them a-special. —Gracious sakes, Henry, you're so tired you can't stand up. Your mother and sister'll be here in a minute and we'll think what to do about you.

HENRY:

What did they ever care about me?

SABINA:

There's that old whine again. All you people think you're not loved enough, nobody loves you. Well, you start being lovable and we'll love you.

HENRY:

Outraged.

I don't want anybody to love me.

SABINA:

Then stop talking about it all the time.

HENRY:

I *never* talk about it. The last thing I want is anybody to pay any attention to me.

SABINA:

I can hear it behind every word you say.

HENRY:

I want everybody to hate me.

SABINA:

Yes, you've decided that's second best, but it's still the same thing. —Mrs. Antrobus! Henry's here. He's so tired he can't stand up.

MRS. ANTROBUS *and* GLADYS, *with her baby, emerge. They are dressed as in Act I.* MRS. ANTROBUS *carries some objects in her apron, and* GLADYS *has a blanket over her shoulder.*

MRS. ANTROBUS *and* GLADYS:

Henry! Henry! Henry!

HENRY:

Glaring at them.

Have you anything to eat?

MRS. ANTROBUS:

Yes, I have, Henry. I've been saving it for this very day—two good baked potatoes. No! Henry! One of them's for your father. Henry!! Give me that other potato back this minute.

SABINA *sidles up behind him and snatches the other potato away.*

SABINA:

He's so dog-tired he doesn't know what he's doing.

MRS. ANTROBUS:

Now you just rest there, Henry, until I can get your room ready. Eat that potato good and slow, so you can get all the nourishment out of it.

HENRY:

You all might as well know right now that I haven't come back here to live.

MRS. ANTROBUS:

Sh. . . . I'll put this coat over you. Your room's hardly damaged at all. Your football trophies are a little tarnished, but Sabina and I will polish them up tomorrow.

HENRY:

Did you hear me? I don't live here. I don't belong to anybody.

MRS. ANTROBUS:

Why, how can you say a thing like that! You certainly do belong right here. Where else would you want to go? Your forehead's feverish, Henry, seems to me. You'd better give me that gun, Henry. You won't need that anymore.

GLADYS:

Whispering.

Look, he's fallen asleep already, with his potato half chewed.

SABINA:

Puh! The terror of the world.

MRS. ANTROBUS:

Sabina, you mind your own business, and start putting the room to rights.

HENRY *has turned his face to the back of the sofa.* MRS. ANTROBUS *gingerly puts the revolver in her apron pocket, then helps* SABINA. SABINA *has found a rope hanging from the ceiling. Grunting, she hangs all her weight on it, and as she pulls, the walls begin to move into their right places.* MRS. ANTROBUS *brings the overturned tables, chairs, and hassock into the positions of Act I.*

SABINA:

That's all we do—always beginning again! Over and over again. Always beginning again.

She pulls on the rope and a part of the wall moves into place. She stops. Meditatively.

How do we know that it'll be any better than before? Why do we go on pretending? Some day the whole earth's going to have to turn cold anyway, and until that time all these other things'll be happening again: it will be more wars and more walls of ice and floods and earthquakes.

MRS. ANTROBUS:

Sabina!! Stop arguing and go on with your work.

SABINA:

All right. I'll go on just out of *habit*, but I won't believe in it.

MRS. ANTROBUS:

Aroused.

Now, Sabina. I've let you talk long enough. I don't want to hear any more of it. Do I have to explain to you what everybody knows, —everybody who keeps a home going? Do I have to say to you what nobody should ever *have* to say, because they can read it in each other's eyes?
Now listen to me:

MRS. ANTROBUS *takes hold of the rope.*

I could live for seventy years in a cellar and make soup out of grass and bark, without ever doubting that this world has a work to do and will do it.
Do you hear me?

SABINA:

Frightened.

Yes, Mrs. Antrobus.

MRS. ANTROBUS:

Sabina, do you see this house, —216 Cedar Street, —do you see it?

SABINA:

Yes, Mrs. Antrobus.

MRS. ANTROBUS:

Well, just to have known this house is to have seen the idea of what we can do someday if we keep our wits about us. Too many people have suffered and died for my children for us to start reneging now. So we'll start putting this house to rights. Now, Sabina, go and see what you can do in the kitchen.

SABINA:

Kitchen! Why is it that however far I go away, I always find myself back in the kitchen?

Exit.

MRS. ANTROBUS:

Still thinking over her last speech, relaxes and speaks, with a reminiscent smile.

Goodness gracious, wouldn't you know that my father was a parson? It was just like I heard his own voice speaking and he's been dead five thousand years. There! I've gone and almost waked Henry up.

HENRY:

Talking in his sleep, indistinctly.

Fellows . . . what have they done for us? . . . Blocked our way at every step. Kept everything in their own hands. And you've stood it. When are you going to wake up?

MRS. ANTROBUS:

Sh, Henry. Go to sleep. Go to sleep. Go to sleep. —Well, that looks better. Now let's go and help Sabina.

GLADYS:

Mama, I'm going out into the backyard and hold the baby right up in the air. And show him that we don't have to be afraid anymore.

Exit GLADYS *to the kitchen.*

MRS. ANTROBUS *glances at* HENRY, *exits into kitchen.*

HENRY *thrashes about in his sleep. Enter* MR. ANTROBUS, *his arms full of bundles, chewing the end of a carrot. He has a slight limp. Over the suit of Act I he is wearing an overcoat too long for him, its skirts trailing on the ground. He lets his bundles fall and stands looking about. Presently his attention is fixed on* HENRY, *whose words grow clearer.*

HENRY:

All right! What have you got to lose? What have they done for us? That's right—nothing. Tear everything down. I don't care what you smash. We'll begin again and we'll show 'em.

MR. ANTROBUS *takes out his revolver and holds it pointing downwards. With his back towards the audience he moves towards the footlights.*

Henry's voice grows louder and he wakes with a start. They stare at one another. Then HENRY *sits up quickly. Throughout the following scene* HENRY *is played, not as a misunderstood or misguided young man, but as a representation of strong unreconciled evil.*

All right! Do something.

Pause.

Don't think I'm afraid of you, either. All right, do what you were going to do. Do it.

Furiously.

Shoot me, I tell you. You don't have to think I'm any relation of yours. I haven't got any father or any mother, or brothers or sisters. And I don't want any. And what's more I haven't got anybody over me; and I never will have. I'm alone, and that's all I want to be: alone. So you can shoot me.

MR. ANTROBUS:

You're the last person I wanted to see. The sight of you dries up all my plans and hopes. I wish I were back at war still, because it's easier to fight you than to live with you. War's a pleasure—do you hear me? —War's a pleasure compared to what faces us now: trying to build up a peacetime with you in the middle of it.

MR. ANTROBUS *walks up to the window.*

HENRY:

I'm not going to be a part of any peacetime of yours. I'm going a long way from here and make my own world that's fit for a man to live in. Where a man can be free, and have a chance, and do what he wants to do in his own way.

MR. ANTROBUS:

His attention arrested; thoughtfully. He throws the gun out of the window and turns with hope.

. . . Henry, let's try again.

HENRY:

Try what? Living *here*? —Speaking polite downtown to all the old men like you? Standing like a sheep at the street corner until the red light turns to green? Being a good boy and a good sheep, like all the stinking ideas you get out of your books? Oh, no. I'll make a world, and I'll show you.

MR. ANTROBUS:

Hard.

How can you make a world for people to live in, unless you've first put order in yourself? Mark my words: I shall continue fighting you until my last breath as long as you mix up your idea of liberty with your idea of hogging everything for yourself. I shall have no pity on you. I shall pursue you to the far corners of the earth. You and I want the same thing; but until you think of it as something that everyone has a right to, you are my deadly enemy and I will destroy you. —I hear your mother's voice in the kitchen. Have you seen her?

HENRY:

I have no mother. Get it into your head. I don't belong here. I have nothing to do here. I have no home.

MR. ANTROBUS:

Then why did you come here? With the whole world to choose from, why did you come to this one place: 216 Cedar Street, Excelsior, New Jersey? . . . Well?

HENRY:

What if I did? What if I wanted to look at it once more, to see if—

MR. ANTROBUS:

Oh, you're related, all right— When your mother comes in you must behave yourself. Do you hear me?

HENRY:

Wildly.

What is this? *—must behave* yourself. Don't you say *must* to me.

MR. ANTROBUS:

Quiet!

Enter MRS. ANTROBUS *and* SABINA.

HENRY:

Nobody can say *must* to me. All my life everybody's been crossing me, —everybody, everything, all of you. I'm going to be free, even if I have to kill half the world for it. Right now, too. Let me get my hands on his throat. I'll show him.

He advances toward MR. ANTROBUS. *Suddenly,* SABINA *jumps between them and calls out in her own person.*

SABINA:

Stop! Stop! Don't play this scene. You know what happened last night. Stop the play.

The men fall back, panting. HENRY *covers his face with his hands.*

Last night you almost strangled him. You became a regular savage. Stop it!

HENRY:

It's true. I'm sorry. I don't know what comes over me. I have nothing against him personally. I respect him very much. . . . I . . . I admire him. But something comes over me. It's like I become fifteen years old again. I . . . I . . . Listen: my own father used to whip me and lock me up every Saturday night. I never had enough to eat. He never let me have enough money to buy decent clothes. I was ashamed to go downtown. I never could go to the dances. My father and my uncle put rules in the way of everything I wanted to do. They tried to prevent my living at all. —I'm sorry. I'm sorry.

MRS. ANTROBUS:

Quickly.

No, go on. Finish what you were saying. Say it all.

HENRY:

In this scene it's as though I were back in high school again. It's like I had some big emptiness inside me, —the emptiness of being hated and blocked at every turn. And the emptiness fills up with the one thought that you have to strike and fight and kill. Listen, it's as though you have to kill somebody else so as not to end up killing yourself.

SABINA:

That's not true. I knew your father and your uncle and your mother. You imagined all that. Why, they did everything they could for you. How can you say things like that? They didn't lock you up.

HENRY:

They did. They did. They wished I hadn't been born.

SABINA:

That's not true.

MR. ANTROBUS:

In his own person, with self-condemnation, but cold and proud.

Wait a minute. I have something to say, too. It's not wholly his fault that he wants to strangle me in this scene. It's my fault, too. He wouldn't feel that way unless there were something in me that reminded him of all that. He talks about an emptiness. Well, there's an emptiness in me, too. Yes, —work, work, work, —that's all I do. I've ceased to *live*. No wonder he feels that anger coming over him.

MRS. ANTROBUS:

There! At least you've said it.

SABINA:

We're all just as wicked as we can be, and that's the God's truth.

MRS. ANTROBUS *nods a moment, then comes forward.*

MRS. ANTROBUS:

Quietly.

Come. Come and put your head under some cold water.

SABINA:

In a whisper.

I'll go with him. I've known him a long while. You have to go on with the play. Come with me.

HENRY *starts out with* SABINA, *but turns at the exit and speaks to* MR. ANTROBUS.

HENRY:

Thanks. Thanks for what you said. I'll be all right tomorrow. I won't lose control in that place. I promise.

Exit HENRY *and* SABINA.

MR. ANTROBUS *starts toward the front door, fastens it.*

MRS. ANTROBUS *goes upstage and places the chair close to table.*

MRS. ANTROBUS:

George, do I see you limping?

MR. ANTROBUS:

Yes, a little. My old wound from the other war started smarting again. I can manage.

MRS. ANTROBUS:

Looking out of the window.

Some lights are coming on, —the first in seven years. People are walking up and down looking at them. Over in Hawkins' open lot they've built a bonfire to celebrate the peace. They're dancing around it like scarecrows.

MR. ANTROBUS:

A bonfire! As though they hadn't seen enough things burning. —Maggie, —the dog died?

MRS. ANTROBUS:

Oh, yes. Long ago. There are no dogs left in Excelsior. —You're back again! All these years. I gave up counting on letters. The few that arrived were anywhere from six months to a year late.

MR. ANTROBUS:

Yes, the ocean's full of letters, along with the other things.

MRS. ANTROBUS:

George, sit down, you're tired.

MR. ANTROBUS:

No, you sit down. I'm tired but I'm restless.

Suddenly, as she comes forward.

Maggie! I've lost it. I've lost it.

MRS. ANTROBUS:

What, George? What have you lost?

MR. ANTROBUS:

The most important thing of all: The desire to begin again, to start building.

MRS. ANTROBUS:

Sitting in the chair right of the table.

Well, it will come back.

MR. ANTROBUS:

At the window.

I've lost it. This minute I feel like all those people dancing around the bonfire—just relief. Just the desire to settle down; to slip into the old grooves and keep the neighbors from walking over my lawn. —Hm. But during the war—in the middle of all that blood and dirt and hot and cold—every day and night, I'd have moments, Maggie, when I *saw* the things that we could do when it was over. When you're at war you think about a better life; when you're at peace you think about a more comfortable one. I've lost it. I feel sick and tired.

MRS. ANTROBUS:

Listen! The baby's crying.

I hear Gladys talking. Probably she's quieting Henry again. George, while Gladys and I were living here—like moles, like rats, and when we were at our wits' end to save the baby's life—the only thought we clung to was that you were going to bring something good out of this suffering. In the night, in the dark, we'd whisper about it, starving and sick. —Oh, George, you'll have to get it back again. Think! What else kept us alive all these years? Even now, it's not comfort we want. We can suffer whatever's necessary; only give us back that promise.

Enter SABINA *with a lighted lamp. She is dressed as in Act I.*

SABINA:

Mrs. Antrobus . . .

MRS. ANTROBUS:

Yes, Sabina?

SABINA:

Will you need me?

MRS. ANTROBUS:

No, Sabina, you can go to bed.

SABINA:

Mrs. Antrobus, if it's all right with you, I'd like to go to the bonfire and celebrate seeing the war's over. And, Mrs. Antrobus, they've opened the Gem Movie Theatre and they're giving away a hand-painted soup tureen to every lady, and I thought one of us ought to go.

MR. ANTROBUS:

Well, Sabina, I haven't any money. I haven't seen any money for quite a while.

SABINA:

Oh, you don't need money. They're taking anything you can give them. And I have some . . . some . . . Mrs. Antrobus, promise you won't tell anyone. It's a little against the law. But I'll give you some, too.

MR. ANTROBUS:

What is it?

SABINA:

I'll give you some, too. Yesterday I picked up a lot of . . . of beef cubes!

MRS. ANTROBUS:

Turns and speaks calmly.

But, Sabina, you know you ought to give that in to the Center downtown. They know who needs them most.

SABINA:

Outburst.

Mrs. Antrobus, I didn't make this war. I didn't ask for it. And, in my opinion, after anybody's gone through what we've gone through, they have a right to grab what they can find. You're a very nice man, Mr. Antrobus, but you'd have got on better in the world if you'd realized that dog-eat-dog was the rule in the beginning and always will be. And most of all now.

In tears.

Oh, the world's an awful place, and you know it is. I used to think something could be done about it; but I know better now. I hate it. I hate it.

She comes forward slowly and brings six cubes from the bag.

All right. All right. You can have them.

MR. ANTROBUS:

Thank you, Sabina.

SABINA:

Can I have . . . can I have one to go to the movies?

MR. ANTROBUS *in silence gives her one.*

Thank you.

MR. ANTROBUS:

Good night, Sabina.

SABINA:

Mr. Antrobus, don't mind what I say. I'm just an ordinary girl, you know what I mean, I'm just an ordinary girl. But you're a bright man, you're a very bright man, and of course you invented the alphabet and the wheel, and, my God, a lot of things . . . and if you've got any other plans, my God, don't let me upset them. Only every now and then I've got to go to the movies. I mean my nerves can't stand it. But if you have any ideas about improving the crazy old world, I'm really with you. I really am. Because it's . . . it's . . . Good night.

She goes out. MR. ANTROBUS *starts laughing softly with exhilaration.*

MR. ANTROBUS:

Now I remember what three things always went together when I was able to see things most clearly: three things. Three things.

He points to where SABINA *has gone out.*

The voice of the people in their confusion and their need. And the thought of you and the children and this house. . . . And . . . Maggie! I didn't dare ask you: my books! They haven't been lost, have they?

MRS. ANTROBUS:

No. There are some of them right here. Kind of tattered.

MR. ANTROBUS:

Yes. —Remember, Maggie, we almost lost them once before? And when we finally did collect a few torn copies out of old cellars they ran in everyone's head like a fever. They as good as rebuilt the world.

Pauses, book in hand, and looks up.

Oh, I've never forgotten for long at a time that living is struggle. I know that every good and excellent thing in the world stands moment by moment on the razor edge of danger and must be fought for—whether it's a field, or a home, or a country. All I ask is the chance to build new worlds and God has always given us that. And has given us

Opening the book.

voices to guide us; and the memory of our mistakes to warn us. Maggie, you and I will remember in peacetime all the resolves that were so clear to us in the days of war. We've come a long ways. We've learned. We're learning. And the steps of our journey are marked for us here.

He stands by the table turning the leaves of a book.

Sometimes out there in the war—standing all night on a hill—I'd try and remember some of the words in these books. Parts of them and phrases would come back to me. And after a while I used to give names to the hours of the night.

He sits, hunting for a passage in the book.

Nine o'clock I used to call Spinoza. Where is it: "After experience had taught me—"

The back wall has disappeared, revealing the platform. FRED BAILEY *carrying his numeral has started from left to right.* MRS. ANTROBUS *sits by the table sewing.*

FRED BAILEY:

"After experience had taught me that the common occurrences of daily life are vain and futile; and I saw that all the objects of my desire and fear were in themselves nothing good nor bad save insofar as the mind was affected by them; I at length determined to search out whether there was something truly good and communicable to man."

Almost without break HESTER, *carrying a large Roman numeral ten, starts crossing the platform.* GLADYS *appears at the kitchen door and moves towards her mother's chair.*

HESTER:

"Then tell me, O Critias, how will a man choose the ruler that shall rule over him? Will he not choose a man who has first established order in himself, knowing that any decision that has its spring from anger or pride or vanity can be multiplied a thousand fold in its effects upon the citizens?"

HESTER *disappears and* IVY, *as eleven o'clock, starts speaking.*

IVY:

"This good estate of the mind possessing its object in energy we call divine. This we mortals have occasionally and it is this energy which is pleasantest and best. But God has it always. It is wonderful in us; but in Him how much more wonderful."

As MR. TREMAYNE *starts to speak,* HENRY *appears at the edge of the scene, brooding and unreconciled, but present.*

MR. TREMAYNE:

"In the beginning, God created the Heavens and the

Earth; And the Earth was waste and void; And the darkness was upon the face of the deep. And the Lord said let there be light and there was light."

Sudden blackout and silence, except for the last strokes of the midnight bell. Then just as suddenly the lights go up, and SABINA *is standing at the window, as at the opening of the play.*

SABINA:

Oh, oh, oh. Six o'clock and the master not home yet. Pray God nothing serious has happened to him crossing the Hudson River. But I wouldn't be surprised. The whole world's at sixes and sevens, and why the house hasn't fallen down about our ears long ago is a miracle to me.

She comes down to the footlights.

This is where you came in. We have to go on for ages and ages yet.

You go home.

The end of this play isn't written yet.

Mr. and Mrs. Antrobus! Their heads are full of plans and they're as confident as the first day they began, —and they told me to tell you: good night.

CURTAIN

This Franklin Library edition of

OUR TOWN *and* THE SKIN OF OUR TEETH

is set in Janson, a typeface first cut

in Amsterdam during the seventeenth century.

The display face, Folkwang, is an exotic

roman typeface created during the 1950s

by Hermann Schardt.

Alan E. Cober's line drawings communicate the

spare realism of Wilder's plays.

The acid-free paper is 60-pound Franklin Library Olde Style Cream,

made to archival standards by the S. D. Warren Paper Company

of Cumberland Mills, Maine, for The Franklin Library.

The book was printed by R. R. Donnelley & Sons Co.,

Chicago, Illinois.